CREATIVE RIBBONWORK

HOW TO MAKE OVER 30 BEAUTIFUL ACCESSORIES AND DECORATIONS

CREATIVE RIBBONWORK

HOW TO MAKE OVER 30 BEAUTIFUL ACCESSORIES AND DECORATIONS

Create your own delightful decorative items using original easy-to-follow ribbonwork projects demonstrated by over 300 stunning colour photographs

LISA BROWN AND CHRISTINE KINGDOM

southwater

This edition is published by Southwater, an imprint of Anness Publishing Ltd, Hermes House, 88–89 Blackfriars Road, London SE1 8HA; tel. 020 7401 2077; fax 020 7633 9499

www.southwaterbooks.com;
www.annesspublishing.com

© Anness Publishing Ltd 2007

If you like the images in this book and would like to investigate using them for publishing, promotions or advertising, please visit our website www.practicalpictures.com for more information.

UK agent: The Manning Partnership Ltd; tel. 01225 478444; fax 01225 478440; sales@manning-partnership.co.uk

UK distributor: Grantham Book Services Ltd; tel. 01476 541080; fax 01476 541061; orders@gbs.tbs-ltd.co.uk

North American agent/distributor: National Book Network; tel. 301 459 3366; fax 301 429 5746; www.nbnbooks.com

Australian agent/distributor: Pan Macmillan Australia; tel. 1300 135 113; fax 1300 135 103; customer.service@macmillan.com.au

New Zealand agent/distributor: David Bateman Ltd; tel. (09) 415 7664; fax (09) 415 8892

Publisher Joanna Lorenz
Editorial Director Helen Sudell
Executive Editor Joanne Rippin
Designer Ian Sandom

ETHICAL TRADING POLICY
Because of our ongoing ecological investment programme, you, as our customer, can have the pleasure and reassurance of knowing that a tree is being cultivated on your behalf to naturally replace the materials used to make the book you are holding. For further information about this scheme, go to www.annesspublishing.com/trees

All rights reserved. No part of this publication may be reproduced, stored in a retrieval system, or transmitted in any way or by any means, electronic, mechanical, photocopying, recording or otherwise, without the prior written permission of the copyright holder.

A CIP catalogue record for this book is available from the British Library.

Previously published as part of a larger volume, *Beadwork and Ribbons*

Contents

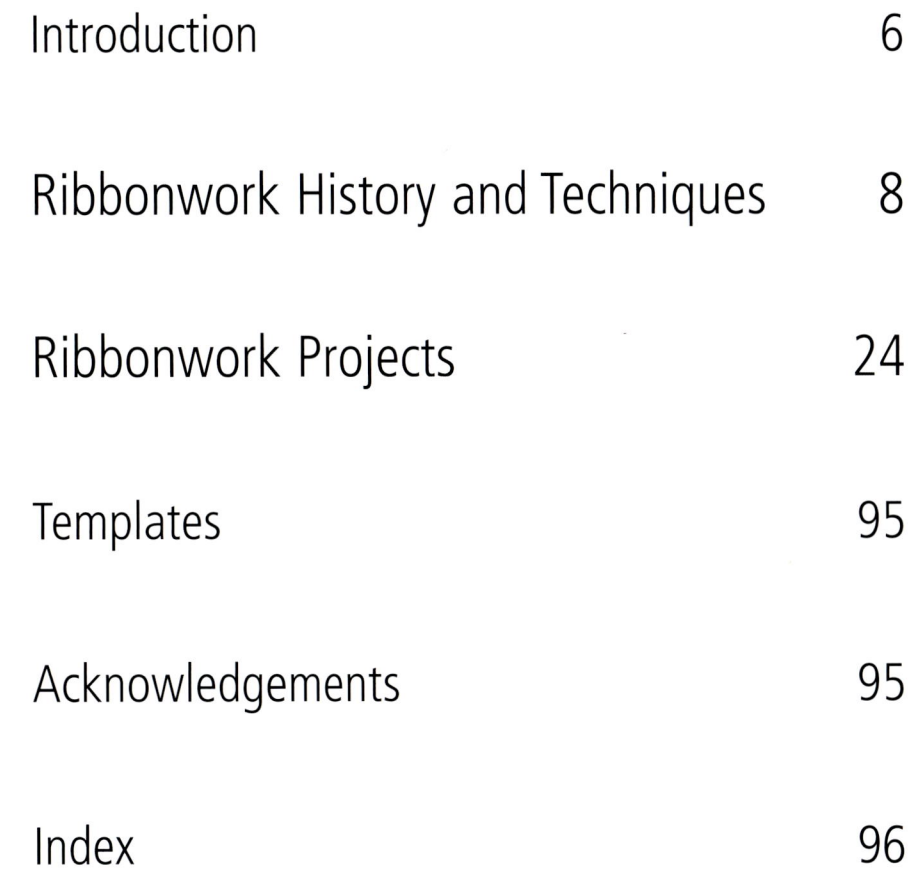

Introduction 6

Ribbonwork History and Techniques 8

Ribbonwork Projects 24

Templates 95

Acknowledgements 95

Index 96

Introduction

Ribbonwork has enjoyed a resurgence in recent years as an ever-growing variety of beautiful fabrics and textures are used in their manufacture. Popular for centuries throughout the world, ribbons have been used for bindings, fastenings and marks of honour, and enjoyed for their beauty and decorative character. The Native American Indians use ribbons extensively in their art, as did the ancient Egyptians, medieval Europeans and the courtiers of Versailles in the early 18th century. From the 1930s ribbons were used less in dress, and also declined as a craft. Today there is a revival in the types of ribbon available, and in the many imaginative and exciting ways to use them.

This book includes ideas from leading designers, with chapters covering fashion accessories and desirable items for the home. An introduction covers all the basic techniques, materials and equipment required, as well as a fascinating history and gallery of styles and inspiration. The projects and ideas that follow are shown with step-by-step instructions that are straightforward and easy to follow, and each project is clearly illustrated. The ●●● symbol indicates how complex a project is. One ● means the project is straightforward and a beginner could tackle it with ease. Projects with ●●● indicate that a more advanced level of skill is required.

The ornamental qualities of ribbons are irresistible. They will add glamour, colour, sparkle and texture to your work, and the creative possibilities are endless.

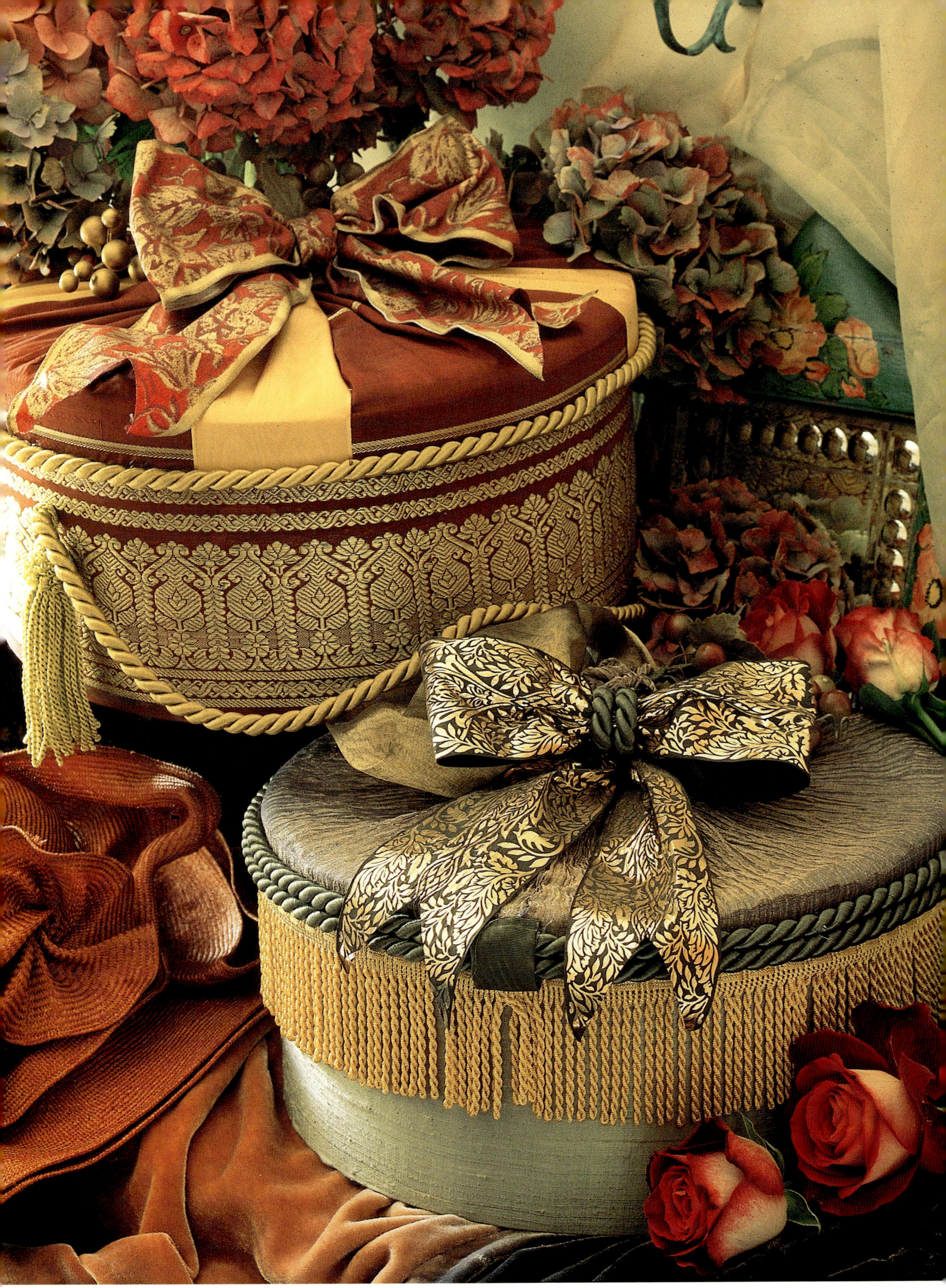

Ribbonwork History and Techniques

For centuries, ribbons were one of the few affordable adornments for all, and from the Middle Ages to the 1800s they were used as fastenings and decorations for garments and hairstyles, crafted into tokens of love and worn as badges of allegiance or awards. From the 1900s ribbon were used less as items of clothing and more as an attractive and widely available craft material. Ribbons in a dazzling variety of colours can now be seen embellishing the smartest gifts, millinery, soft furnishings and fashionable outfits.

The History of Ribbons

From the very earliest times, ribbons have served both practical and decorative purposes. The history of the ribbon is closely aligned to the history of fashion, but its use and popularity has changed dramatically.

The earliest examples of ribbons – in the broad sense of narrow strips of fabric – are from ancient Egypt and can be dated to about 3000BC. It is impossible to say for certain how or where weaving was first developed, but, having produced lengths of fabric, people began to use them as clothing, and embellished them in various ways.

During the Middle Ages, a variety of elaborate borders began to be used to decorate clothing. In England, gowns had become relatively complex garments. The bodice was slit down either side from arm to hip and fitted with ribbons, which were used to tie the material tightly across the upper part of the body. By the middle of the 12th century, skirts had become fuller with dozens of knife-pleats, and the tightness of the bodice was accentuated with a belt resembling a deep cummerbund, which was tied at the back with ribbons.

By the 16th century, trade with the New World had developed and a middle class emerged, eager to spend its wealth on imitating the style of the aristocracy. Henry VIII loved richly decorated garments and headdresses and, to protect himself and the Court from being copied, he introduced legislation preventing anyone but royalty and the aristocracy from wearing decorative embroidery, ribbons woven with gold and silver thread, brocades and jewellery.

The use of ribbons and other adornments was relatively modest during the Puritan period of the 17th century, but the restoration of the English monarchy in 1660 and the coming of age of France's Sun King, Louis XIV, in 1661 brought about a complete change of attitude in both countries. Louis XIV's powerful and dazzling court in France and the self-indulgent rule of Charles II in England were reflected in the costume of men and women. Men's petticoat-breeches, doublets and shoes were decorated all over with bunches of ribbon. Tight stockings were generally pulled over the breeches and fastened with a garter, which was also decorated with a bunch of ribbons. Women's skirts were divided or drawn up with lavishly tied ribbon to reveal extremely ornate petticoats beneath.

The Court of Versailles dominated all matters of taste and fashion among the European aristocracy in the early 18th century. At the same time, the middle classes experienced increasing

Below: A pedlar selling ribbons. A travelling salesman would bring his wares to isolated farms and villages.

Above: This Flemish woman from the 17th century wears a dress embellished with huge silk ribbon bows.

Right: The interior of Hill Bros Millinery Goods in the 19th century, with hundreds of rolls of ribbon for hat trimming.

prosperity and for the first time fashion became the domain of the majority. Ribbons played an essential role, being used to trim gowns and bonnets, tie up hair for a ball, lace dainty shoes and in the form of waistbands, sashes, frills, favours and rosettes. Children were smothered in ribbon, and curtains and cushions were embellished with broad bands of silk. Ribbons were produced in a dazzling variety of weaves and colours; plain, striped, checked, watered, shot, shaded and figured ribbons were all widely available. During the Napoleonic wars, weavers were recruited for the army, leaving the trade short of labour. The smuggling of vast quantities of French ribbon almost became an industry in itself in coastal villages, and yet the demand was still not met.

In 1813, a scalloped-edged ribbon became the rage and weavers had never known a time of such fierce demand for their product. In London, for a period of two years while the craze lasted, manufacturers could ask whatever prices they wished.

By the first half of the 19th century, the Industrial Revolution was in full swing and fashion was no longer dictated by nobility. Department stores sprang up in all major cities and off-the-peg clothes appeared for the first time. Parasols, large-brimmed hats and the new fashion accessory, the handbag, were all extravagantly decorated with rosettes and bows.

In 1823, jacquard looms were introduced in Coventry, thus extending the variety of fancy ribbons available. Ribbon factories and mills were built, all making use of steam-powered looms, although workers using hand looms still continued their trade, particularly in the countryside. The increased prosperity of the time meant that working girls had a little money to indulge in a piece of ribbon to trim a hat, and Coventry found a new middle- and lower-class market.

The period between 1850 and 1870 was one of unprecedented prosperity for an enormous number of people. Women's clothes became increasingly complex, made from two or three different materials and trimmed with a medley of folds, frills and pleats. Ribbons and braids were an integral part of the garments, and by the 1880s, bustles became known as the "upholstered style" because they were made from draperies more suited to furnishing a room than trimming a dress. The turn of the 20th century saw a general softening of the silhouette and tucks, frills, ruchings and other ribbon trims were gradually modified. As the size and complexity of dresses diminished, hats grew larger and were trimmed with a profusion of ribbons and feathers. These extravagant hats gradually gave way to more modest creations: the cloche hat of the 1920s was quite plain but often trimmed with a fancy rosette on one side.

From the 1930s until quite recently, the significance of the ribbon as a fashion item diminished, with just the occasional reappearance as trends dictated – during the 1960s for example. There is today a revival of interest in ribbons and ribboncrafts, although the emphasis is now as much on home decoration as on fashion. Ribbon embroidery is the new stitchcraft and ribbon weaving, pleating, plaiting and ruching are all being rediscovered.

ribbonwork history and techniques

Ribbons are an extremely versatile medium and presented here is a selection of work by contemporary designers that illustrates just some of the wide range of effects that can be achieved.

Gallery of Ribbonwork

Textile artists working in techniques from weaving and stitching to leatherwork and millinery are today using lengths of ribbons on their own to create texture and pattern, or in small amounts to add colourful detail to their designs. The simplicity of the ribbon hat, top right, makes the most of the natural flow of coiled ribbon, and the woven cushion overleaf exploits the subtle shades of soft velvet, whilst the gloves and hydrangea picture show a more traditional use of ribbon as embellishment.

Below: WAVES WALL HANGING
Ribbon makes an ideal material for weaving, and offers dramatic effects. The inspiration for this design came from the shapes that are created by the weaving techniques employed. Small-scale undulations, or waves, are produced through the interaction of the bands of a thick wool warp and thin ribbon weft.
PATRICIA TINDALE

Below: CHRISTENING GOWN
Double-face satin ribbon to match the cream lace has been appliquéd on to the gown using various simple techniques.
JENNY BANHAM

Above: RIBBON SPIRAL HAT
This elegant ribbon hat was inspired by the natural way in which the ribbon spirals when pulled from the roll.
JO BUCKLER

Right: EMBROIDERED GLOVES
These hand-stitched gloves, which are embroidered with ribbons, are based on an original 17th-century pair. The decoration is typical of the period when ribbons were used in profusion.
PAMELA WOODS

Right: RIBBON EMBROIDERY
This beautiful embroidery was inspired by the pretty, delicately coloured hydrangea. It is composed mainly of machine embroidery with ribbon embellishment. First the bracts were drawn, outlined and shaded in. Then the tiny flowers were worked by hand using ribbon, beads and French knots. The foliage was machined without any further drawing on to the fabric.
DAPHNE J. ASHBY

14 ribbonwork history and techniques

Left: INVITATION
This card was made by drawing a decorative border of delicate roses on to parchment paper. It was then colour-washed in watercolour before being decorated with ribbon rosebuds and bows.
LINDSAY CHALFORD BROWN

Above WOVEN CUSHION
The charm and beauty of this woven cushion lies in the fantastic colour scheme and texture of the velvet ribbons.
HIKARU NOGUCHI

Below: AFRICAN HANGING
This wall hanging was made by stitching together two layers of simple patchwork in a grid pattern. Selected areas of the patchwork were then cut away to reveal the layer underneath. The surface was covered with couched "ribbons" of hand-dyed silk to create geometric patterns.
JENNY CHIPPINDALE

Above: TREASURE CHEST
The lid of the chest is made up of a square of ribbon weaving worked in fine ribbons in shades of blue. It is enhanced with extra ribbons, held in place with single strands of metallic embroidery thread, worked in cross stitch and French knots. To give a three-dimensional effect, the weaving was mounted on to card. This shape suggested the lid of a treasure chest, inspiring the designer to make the rest of the chest.
M. MAUREEN VOISEY

Equipment

A simple sewing kit of needles, thread and scissors is all that you need for basic ribbonwork, but a few of the projects that follow require more specialized items, which are readily available from craft suppliers.

Above: Equipment such as a glue gun, florist's tape and stub wire is required for a few of the projects in the book. However, for many of them a good range of sewing equipment is all that is needed.

Dressmaker's chalk

This makes an easily removed line to mark templates or specific intervals on to fabric or ribbon.

Dressmaker's pins

Long, straight pins have many uses in ribbonwork. Glass- or pearl-headed versions are easier to handle and are used for weaving.

Florist's tape (stem wrap)

Flexible and stretchy, this green self-sticking tape is used to conceal wire stems and bind the stems of fresh flowers together.

Glue

Although not essential, a glue gun will quickly become indispensable once purchased. They apply glue with speed and accuracy, even in tricky areas, and are available in various sizes. A small gun is ideal for beginners. As with any adhesive product, it is important to keep glue guns out of the reach of children. PVA or white craft glue is ideal for larger-scale sticking and dries clear. Double-sided tape is good for paper projects and gives a neat finish.

Sewing thread

Polyester thread comes in a wide range of colours, so you should always be able to find a reel to match the ribbon you are using.

Scissors

Use small, sharp-bladed scissors for trimming thread and cutting ribbons, and larger dressmaking shears for fabric. Keep a third pair especially for cutting paper only.

Stub (floral) wire

Florists use this thick, straight wire for supporting the flower stems. It is used to make the stalks of ribbon roses.

Tape measure

This is useful for checking the length of ribbons before cutting and also for measuring the progress of bead weaving, bracelets or necklaces.

Weaving board

A heat-resistant, fabric-covered soft board that will take pins easily is needed for weaving, although an ironing board is a good substitute.

Wire cutters

An essential tool for cutting florist's and stub wire. Some pliers, such as those illustrated here, can be used to cut wire, as well as to shape it.

Ribbons come in myriad textures, colours and widths, and there is a ribbon for every occasion and season, from baby pastels and frothy sheers to designer prints and brocades.

Types of Ribbon

Cut-edge craft
This ribbon is made from a wide fabric and then cut into strips. It is available wired or unwired and is suitable only for craft applications. The special finish stops the ribbon from fraying but means it is not washable.

Grosgrain
These ribbons have a distinctive crosswise rib and are a stronger, denser weave than most other ribbon types. Grosgrains are made in solid colours, stripes, dots and prints; satin and grosgrain combinations are also available.

Jacquards
An intricate pattern is incorporated in the weave of the ribbon. This can be multicoloured or single-colour combinations, florals or geometric patterns, which give a beautiful tapestry-like effect.

Lace-edged satins and jacquards
These are sometimes embellished with a lace edge that is stitched or bonded on to the selvedge. It is particularly popular for bridal applications.

Merrow-edge
This describes the fine satin-stitched edge, usually incorporating a wire, that is added to elaborate cut-edge ribbons for stability and decoration. It is often in lurex thread but can also be in a contrasting colour.

Metallics
These ribbons are made from or incorporate metallic or pearlized fibres. Many different weaves and finishes result in a number of combinations.

Moiré
This effect is the result of a water-mark finish applied during manufacture. It gives a lustrous finish.

Ombré taffeta
A finely woven taffeta with colour shading across the width. Variations include plaids and interesting colour blends giving a lustrous finish and subtle tonal effects.

Plaids and checks
Popular classics, plaids and checks are usually taffeta weaves but are also available in cut-edge ribbon.

Satins
Satins are either double-face or single-face. They are available in plain colours or printed. Some incorporate edgings such as picot- or feather-edge.

Sheers
These fine, almost transparent ribbons are available as plain ribbons or with satin, lurex or jacquard stripes. A thicker yarn is used along the selvedge to give stability. This is known as a monofilament edge.

Shot-effect taffeta
The use of different, often contrasting colours for the warp and weft results in a shot effect giving a really lustrous, colour-shaded finish, similar to shot silk. This product is available both wired and unwired.

Velvets
The deep, plush pile of velvet is unmistakable and the depth of colour is exceptional. Imitation velvets are also available.

Wire-edged taffeta
A fine weave with a matt rather than shiny finish. This product looks the same on both sides and is available plain or with lurex incorporated. Weaves include plaids, checks and ombrés. Taffeta can also be printed or given a shimmering watermark finish. The wire-edge is usually encased so it is not visible.

Woven-edge ribbon
These ribbons are woven in narrow strips, with a non-fraying selvedge running along both edges. They are ideal for projects that need to be laundered or that will have heavy wear. The ribbon reels should carry laundry instructions and details of crease resistance and colour fastness.

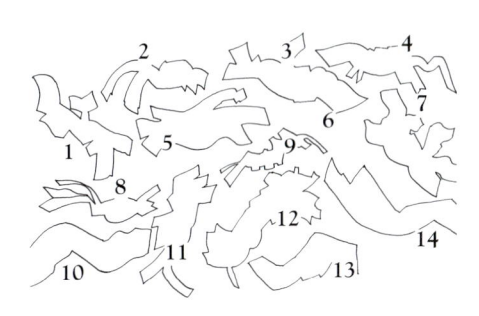

Ribbon Conversions

1.5mm (1/16in)	36mm (1 3/8in)
3mm (1/8in)	39mm (1 1/2in)
5mm (3/16in)	50mm (2in)
7mm (1/4in)	56mm (2 1/4in)
9mm (3/8in)	67mm (2 5/8in)
12mm (1/2in)	70mm (2 3/4in)
15mm (5/8in)	77mm (3in)
23mm (7/8in)	80mm (3 1/4in)
25mm (1in)	

1 Ombré taffeta; 2 Grosgrain; 3 Sheer; 4 Jaquard; 5 Wire-edged taffeta; 6 Lace-edged; 7 Shot-effect taffeta; 8 Plaid and check; 9 Velvet; 10 Merrow-edge; 11 Moiré; 12 Metallic; 13 Cut-edge craft; 14 Satin

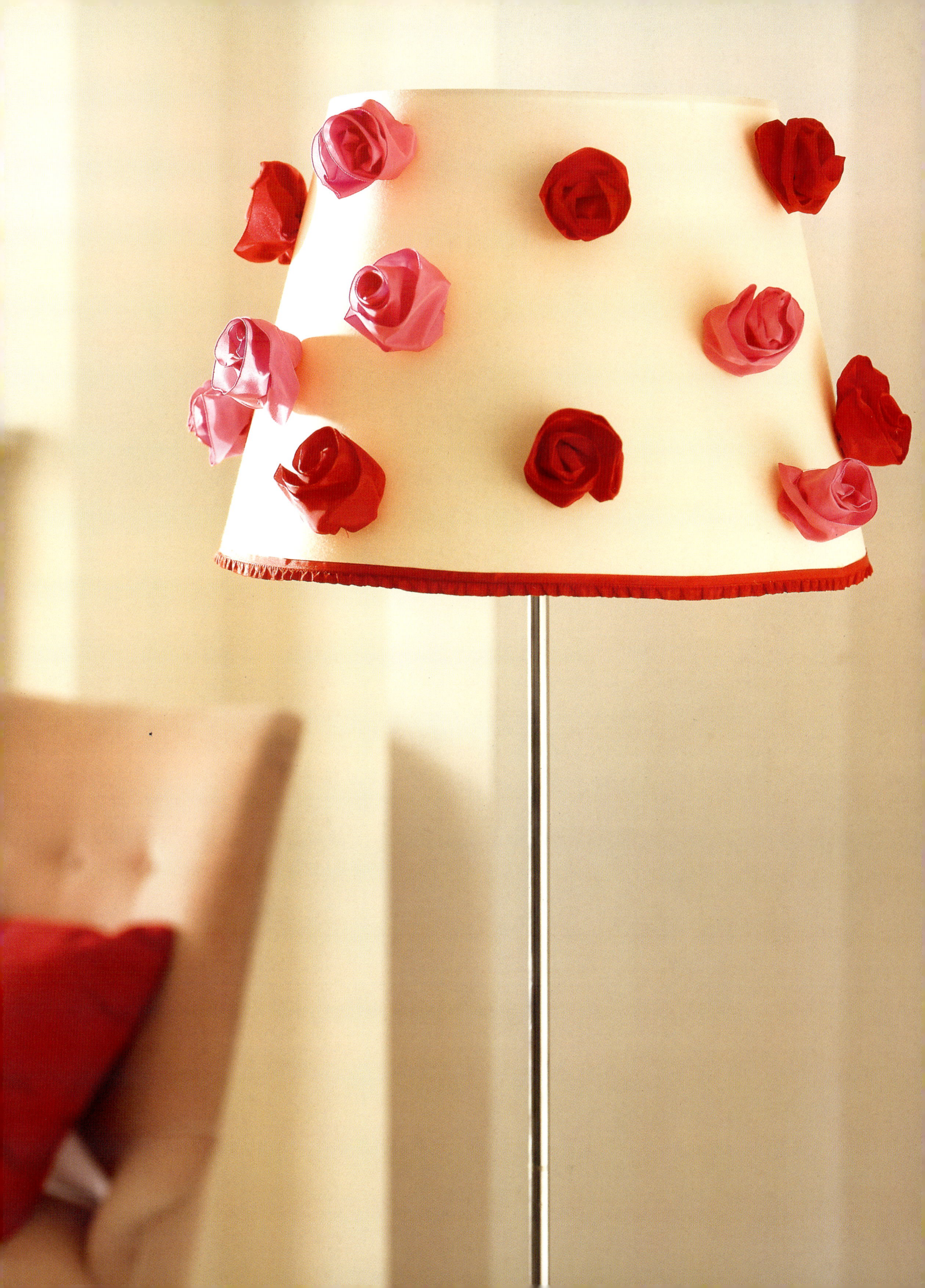

ribbonwork projects

Glamorize plain bedlinen by edging a pile of pillows with ribbon bands and bows. Bright ginghams work well in a child's bedroom, but you could adapt the idea using cooler colours for a more sophisticated look.

Pillowcase Edgings

you will need
Plain white cotton pillowcases
Plain and gingham ribbons of various widths
Tape measure
Scissors
Fusible bonding web
Iron
Needle and matching thread
Dressmaker's pins

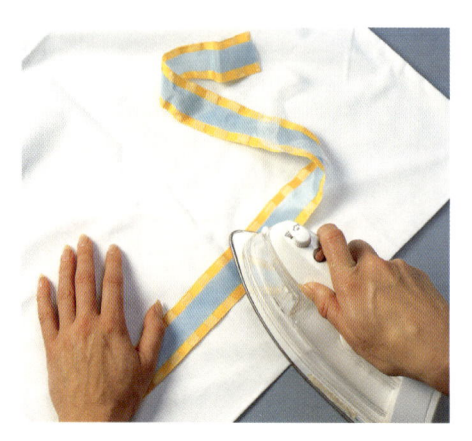

1 For the banded pillowcase, cut lengths of three different ribbons about 5cm/2in longer than the width of the pillowcase. Cut three lengths of fusible bonding web to size and use to attach each of the ribbons.

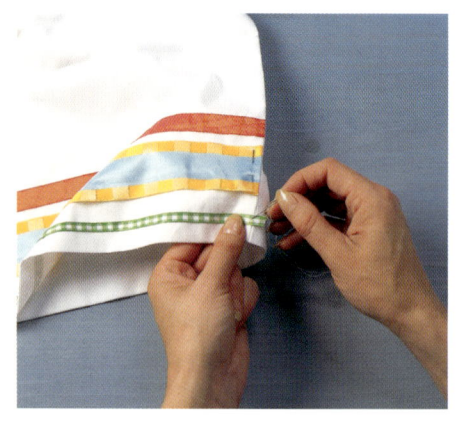

2 Turn in the raw edges and stitch the ribbons to the pillowcase at each end. Hand sew with tiny stitches along each long edge of the pillowcase.

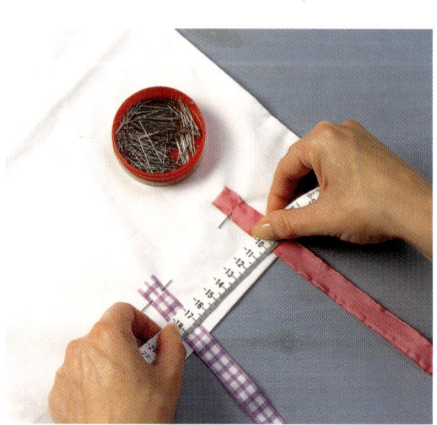

3 For the pillowcase with ties, cut two 30cm/12in lengths from each of five different narrow ribbons and pin one of each pair at regular intervals along the folded edge of the pillowcase opening. Stitch in place at the ends.

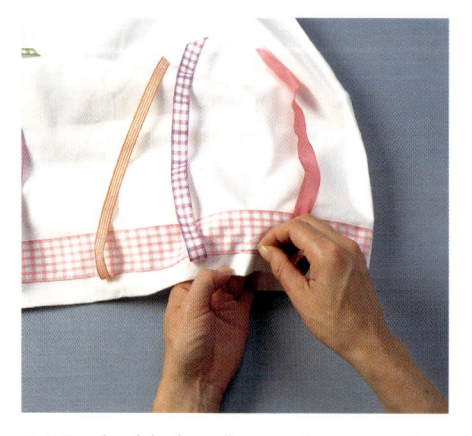

4 Use fusible bonding web to attach a length of wide ribbon to conceal the stitched ends of the ties. Hand or machine stitch around all four edges.

5 Attach the matching ribbon lengths to the other side of the pillowcase opening, folding in the raw edges and stitching neatly to secure.

pillowcase edgings **33**

6 To decorate the pillowcase with ties, cut lengths of ribbon of differing widths and pin them across the corners. Slip stitch to secure.

7 Fold the loose ends to the back of the pillowcase. Cut a second length of each ribbon, tuck under the ends to conceal the raw edges and slip stitch in place.

8 Finish the corner with a small ribbon bow, stitched through the knot to prevent it from coming undone.

The pleasure given by your gifts will be doubled when they are presented in these gorgeous wrappings. Plain boxes – new or recycled – can be painted brightly and adorned with ribbons to suit any occasion.

Gift Boxes

you will need
Wire-edged shot-taffeta ribbons in various widths
Gift boxes
Scissors
Tape measure
PVA (white) glue
Needle and matching threads

Red gift box

1 Cut a 105cm/41in length of 4cm/1½in ribbon and fold into seven 15cm/6in concertina pleats. Trim the ribbons into chevrons. Carefully cut a small nick in the centre of each long side and tie a small piece of ribbon around the middle to secure the loops.

2 Open out each fold to make a rounded loop. Hold the bow in place on the gift box lid. Tuck the ends of the ribbon under the box lid and glue in place. Cut off the excess ribbon.

Large purple gift box

Cut four lengths of green ribbon. Wrap each length around one side of the box and tie in a single loop bow at one corner. Slip each new ribbon under the previous bow. Cut the end of each ribbon into a chevron.

Green gift box

1 Wrap a length of purple wire-edged shot-taffeta ribbon around the gift box and cut off, leaving a little extra for tying a knot. Fold the ribbon into small pleats widthways at regular intervals. Secure the pleats with neat stitches in matching thread.

2 Wrap the ribbon around the box, gluing in place at the points where the ribbon is tied. Tie the ribbon in a knot close to one corner of the box and cut the ribbon ends in chevrons.

Small purple gift box

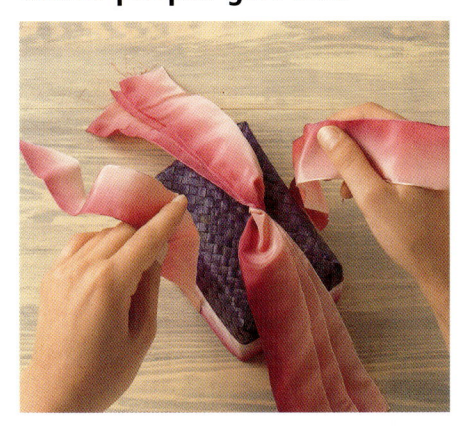

1 Glue a length of pink ribbon around the edge of the lid. Cut two equal lengths of ribbon and glue one end of each to the inside of the lid on opposite sides. Cut three 38cm/15in lengths of ribbon and twist together in the middle. Place the twist in the centre of the lid and tie the two glued ribbons together over the twisted ribbons.

2 Making sure that the ends are all level, tie all eight ribbons together with an overhand knot. Cut the ends at a diagonal angle and ease the ribbons apart to give depth to the trim.

Dark purple gift box

Cut two lengths of pink ribbon. Tie one length around the box in one direction and the other ribbon in the opposite direction. Holding the ribbons together in pairs, fasten in a single-loop bow. Pull the loops and tails apart. Cut the extending ribbon ends into chevrons.

ribbonwork projects

Pamper yourself with these co-ordinating accessories – easily and quickly made by adding pretty ribbons to bathroom basics – but don't forget to check that both the ribbon and accessory are washable.

Bathroom Set

you will need

White hand towel:
Dressmaker's pins
Tape measure
Crewel needle
Red double-face satin ribbon, 3.5m x 3mm/4yd x ⅛in
Scissors

Black mesh container:
Dressmaker's pins
Tape measure
Red spotted double-face satin ribbon, 11.75m x 3mm/13yd x ⅛in
Red double-face satin ribbon, 1.5m x 3mm/1⅔yd x ⅛in
Small red starfish
PVA (white) glue
Scissors
Crewel needle
Needle and matching threads

Wash mitt:
Black spotted double-face satin ribbon, 25cm x 1cm/10 x ½in
Scissors
Needle and matching thread
Black spotted ribbon, 1.5m x 2.5cm/1½yd x 1in

White hand towel

Place pins 2.5cm/1in apart along all four edges of the towel. Thread a crewel needle with the red ribbon. Insert the needle at one pin and bring it out at the next. Knot the ends of the ribbon together neatly so that the ribbon lies flat against the towel. Cut off the excess ribbon, leaving short tails.

Black mesh container

1 Decorate the rim of the lid and base of the container with the spotted ribbon, as for the towel. Glue the starfish around the sides.

2 To make a tassel, bunch together 26 x 38cm/15in lengths of red spotted ribbon. Cut two 30cm/12in lengths of the red ribbon. Fold one length in half and wrap it around the middle of the bunch. Thread the ends through the loop and pull tightly.

Wash mitt

Cut a length of 1cm/⅓in black spotted ribbon to fit the strap, adding an extra 1cm/½in. Turn under 6mm/¼in at each end and stitch the ribbon to the strap. Cut three long lengths of 2.5cm/1in black spotted ribbon. Place them on top of each other and tie in a bow around the strap.

3 Thread a crewel needle with the remaining ribbon. Bind it tightly around the tassel, then slip the needle behind the binding ribbon and pull tightly. Trim the tassel ends level, then sew it to the centre of the lid.

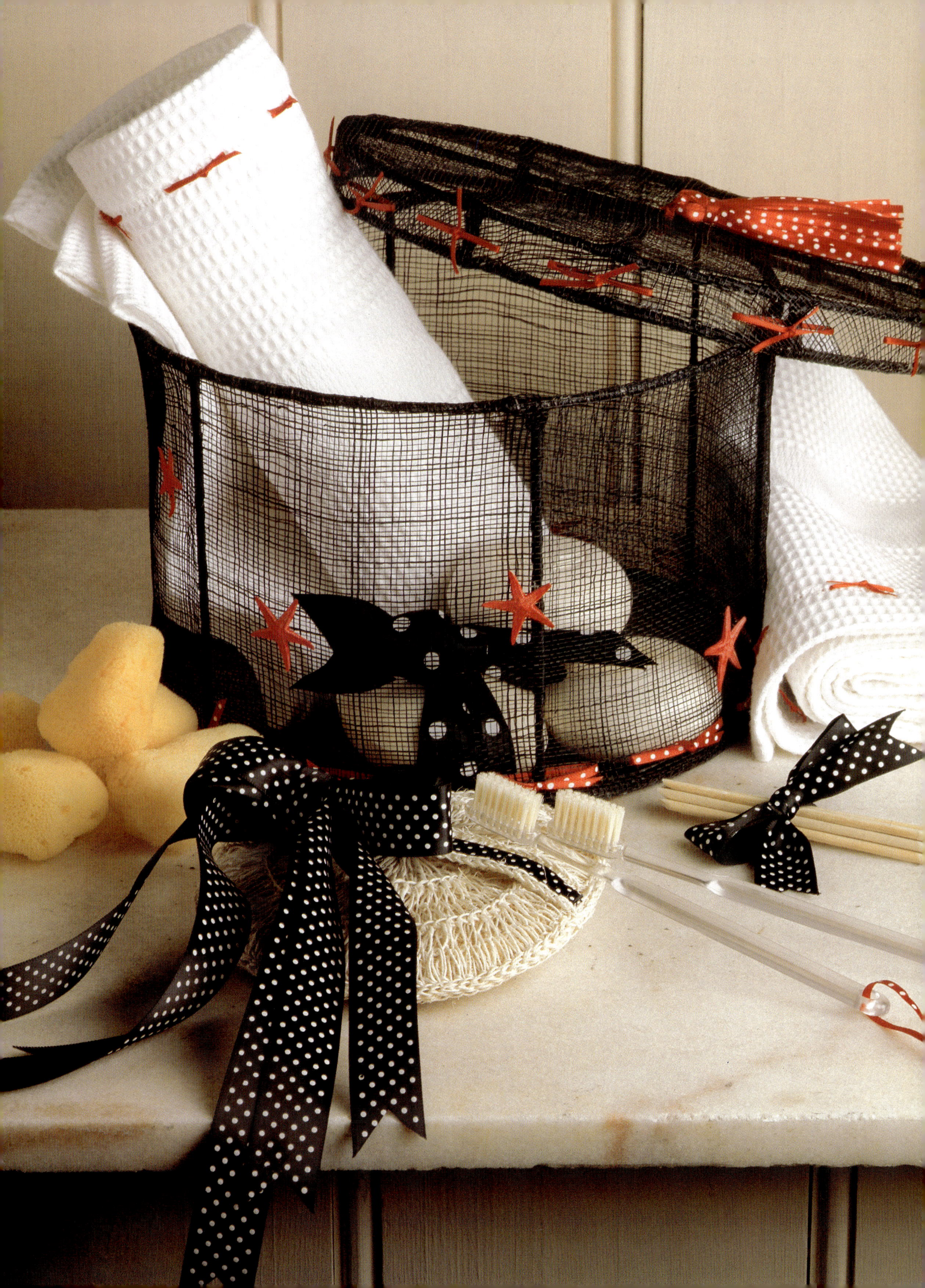

# Ribbon-embroidered Bag

This project uses simple ribbon-embroidered flowers to great effect. To vary the bag, embroider multi-coloured flowers directly on to striped cotton and tie with matching ribbon.

you will need

White loose-weave waffle fabric, 30 x 25cm/12 x 10in
Embroidery hoop
Deep blue, pink, purple and yellow satin ribbons, 1m x 3mm/1yd x ⅛in of each
Chenille needle
Iron
Scissors
Emerald green satin ribbon, 70cm x 3mm/27½ x ⅛in
Bright blue satin ribbon, 1.75m x 3mm/2yd x ⅛in
Green and white striped fabric, 25 x 13cm/10 x 5in
Dressmaker's pins
Matching thread
Pot pourri

1 Place the fabric in an embroidery hoop. Starting 10cm/4in in from one long edge, work a row of eight lazy daisy stitch flowers in deep blue, pink, purple and yellow ribbon (see Basic Techniques) over 20cm/8in. Space them evenly and make each flower 2cm/¾in in diameter. Work a French knot in the centre of each flower.

2 Press the fabric lightly and trim to 25 x 20cm/10 x 8in so the flowers lie 7.5cm/3in from the bottom. Thread the needle with emerald green ribbon and weave two horizontal lines through the top threads of the fabric to form a border on either side of the flowers. With bright blue ribbon, weave seven vertical lines.

3 Pin and stitch the green and white fabric along the top edge of the waffle fabric, right sides facing, with a 1cm/½in seam allowance. Open out and press the seam. Fold in half vertically, right sides of the lining facing. Pin and stitch a side seam along the edge.

4 Pin and stitch along the bottom edge. Clip the corners and turn right-side out. Push the green lining to the inside and press the top edge. Fill with pot pourri. Complete by tying the remaining ribbons into a bow around the neck of the bag.

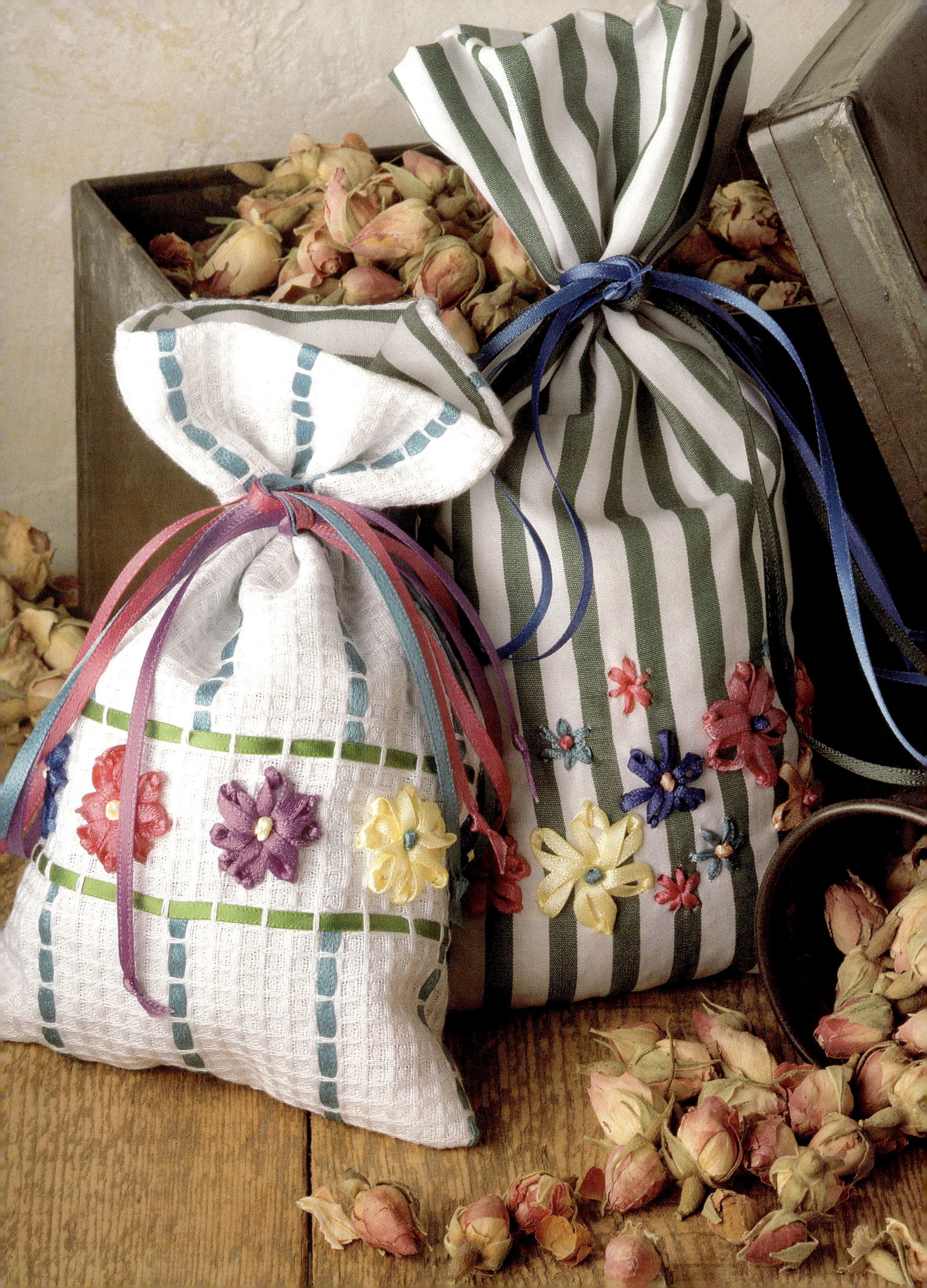

Inspired by fond memories of 1950s raffia baskets, this design uses ribbon embroidery to emblazon a plain shopping basket with a scattering of simple coloured daisies.

Embroidered Basket

you will need
Thin card (stock)
Pencil
Craft (utility) knife
Fabric marker
Straw basket
Large-eyed tapestry needle
Narrow embroidery ribbons
Needle and matching threads
Matchstick (wooden match)

1 Cut out the template at the back of the book from card. Following the main picture as a guide, mark two rows of flowers around the basket, changing the angle of each one as you work, to give variety to the pattern.

2 Thread the tapestry needle with green ribbon, then make a long stitch from one end of the stem to the other. Finish off with a knot on the wrong side. Using a sewing needle and matching thread, couch down the ribbon along the marked line with small straight stitches.

3 To make the centre of the flower, thread the tapestry needle with a length of ribbon and make a small stitch over a matchstick. Do not pull the ribbon tight. Make a second small stitch over the matchstick and then remove it. Work five more "knots" around the centre.

4 For the petals, thread the tapestry needle with ribbon and knot the end. Insert the needle on the wrong side and bring it out next to the centre knots. Insert the needle at the same point and return to the wrong side leaving a loop about 2.5cm/1in long.

5 Thread a sewing needle with matching thread and, bringing it out to the right side at the tip of the petal, sew down the loop. Repeat all around the flower. Continue stitching the flowers until the bag is complete.

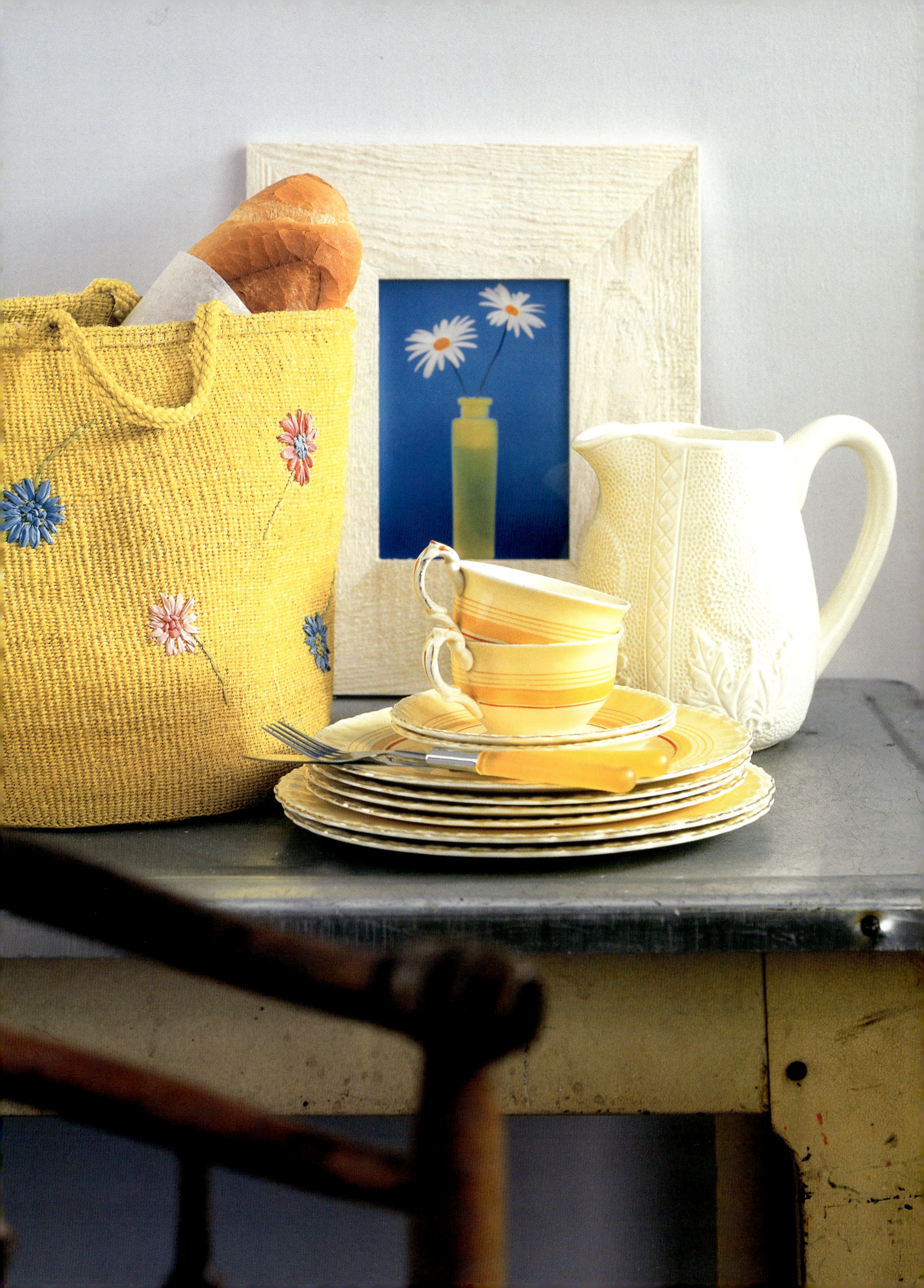

Trimming is the main function of ribbon, and here a plain place mat is transformed to brighten up a simple table setting. As with any other item that will be laundered, check the ribbon is washable.

Ribbon Table Mats

you will need
Woven table mats
Ruler
Contrasting grosgrain ribbon, 1cm/½in wide
Contrasting checked ribbon, 2.5cm/1in wide
Toning grosgrain ribbon, 15mm/⅝in wide
Scissors
Dressmaker's pins
Needle and contrasting and matching threads
Iron and damp cloth

1 Calculate the ribbon requirements by measuring all around the edges of the table mats, adding 20cm/8in for turnings. Cut each colour of ribbon into four lengths, one for each edge of the mat plus a 2.5cm/1in turning allowance at each end.

2 Starting from the outside edge, lay the ribbons in place around the mat. Use the ruler to ensure the ribbons are parallel to the edge. Pin each one in place, leaving the ends free.

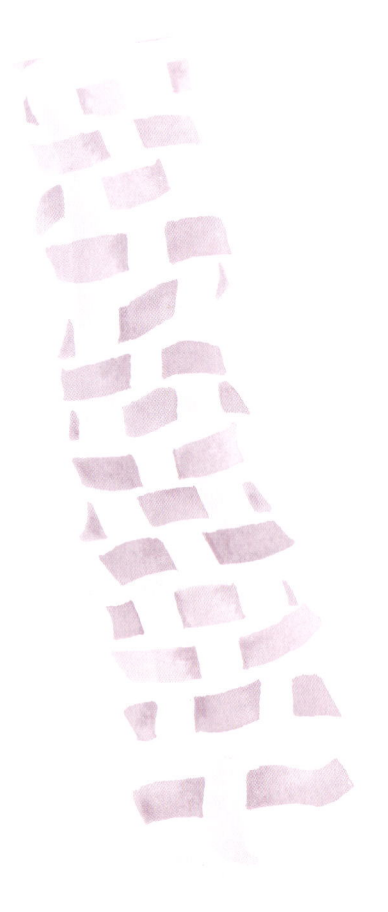

3 Interlace the ribbons to produce a woven effect where they meet and overlap at the corners and pin in place. Tack (baste) them down with contrasting thread and remove the pins.

4 Sew the ribbons down with matching thread using an invisible slip stitch along each edge, working the stitches closely together. Turn under the raw ends and sew to the back of the table mat. Press the piece under a damp cloth with the right side down.

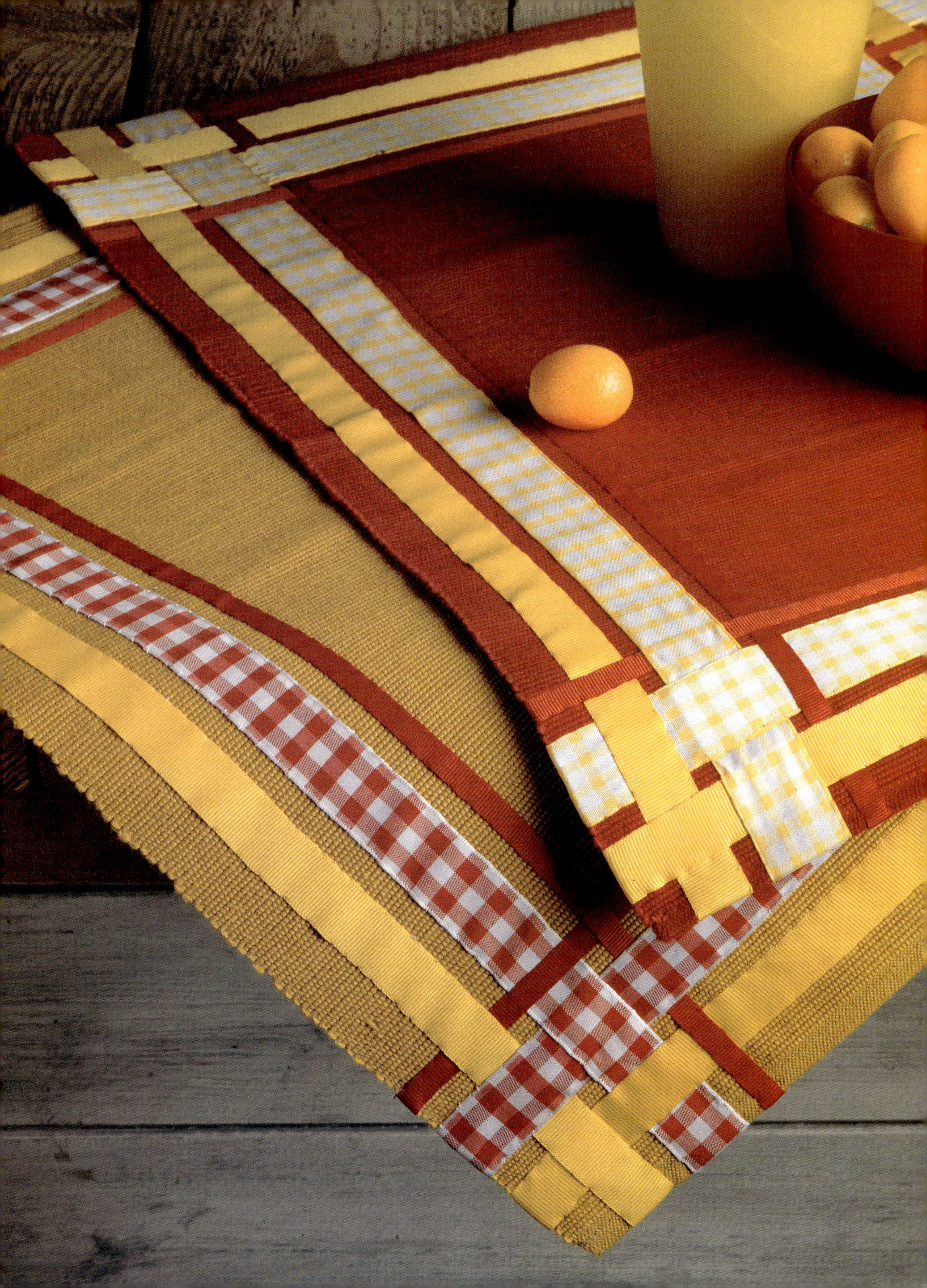

44 ribbonwork projects

Let fresh air in and keep flies out with a brilliant Mexican-style curtain. Each length ends with a large glass bead to add weight and substance: the number required depends on the width of the door frame.

Ribbon Door Curtain

you will need
Tape measure
Length of 2.5 x 2.5cm/1 x 1in wooden batten (furring strip)
Hacksaw
Drill and drill bit
Ruler
Pencil
Double-face satin ribbon in six bright colours, 15mm/⅝in wide
Scissors
Coloured glass disc-shaped beads
Staple gun
2 wood screws
Screwdriver

1 Measure the width of your door frame. Mark the distance on the wooden batten, then use the hacksaw to cut it to the correct length. It should fit snugly inside the top of the door frame.

2 Draw a pencil line along the centre of the batten. Make a mark every 2.5cm/1in along the batten to indicate the positions where the ribbons will be attached. Drill a hole through the mark closest to each end to hold the screws.

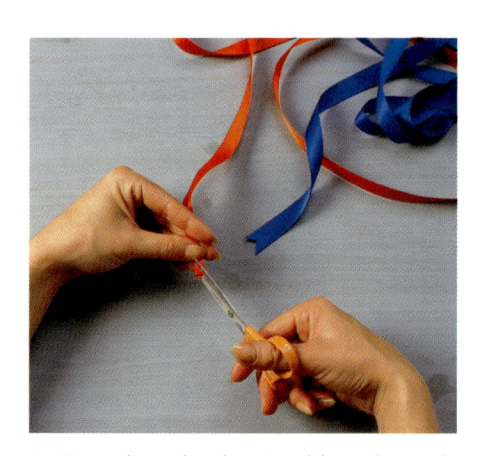

3 Cut a length of satin ribbon for each point marked on the batten, about 15cm/6in longer than the door measurement to allow for attachment and tying on the glass beads. Trim one end of each length into neat points.

4 Fold the trimmed end over for about 10cm/4in, then push the folded end through the hole in the centre of a glass bead. Pull the whole length of the ribbon through the loop and pull taut to hold the bead securely. Repeat with all the ribbon lengths.

5 Fold under 15mm/⅝in at the other end of each ribbon and staple to the batten at a pencil mark, checking they are all the same length as you go. Follow the same colour sequence all across the curtain. Finally, attach the batten to the door frame with two long woodscrews.

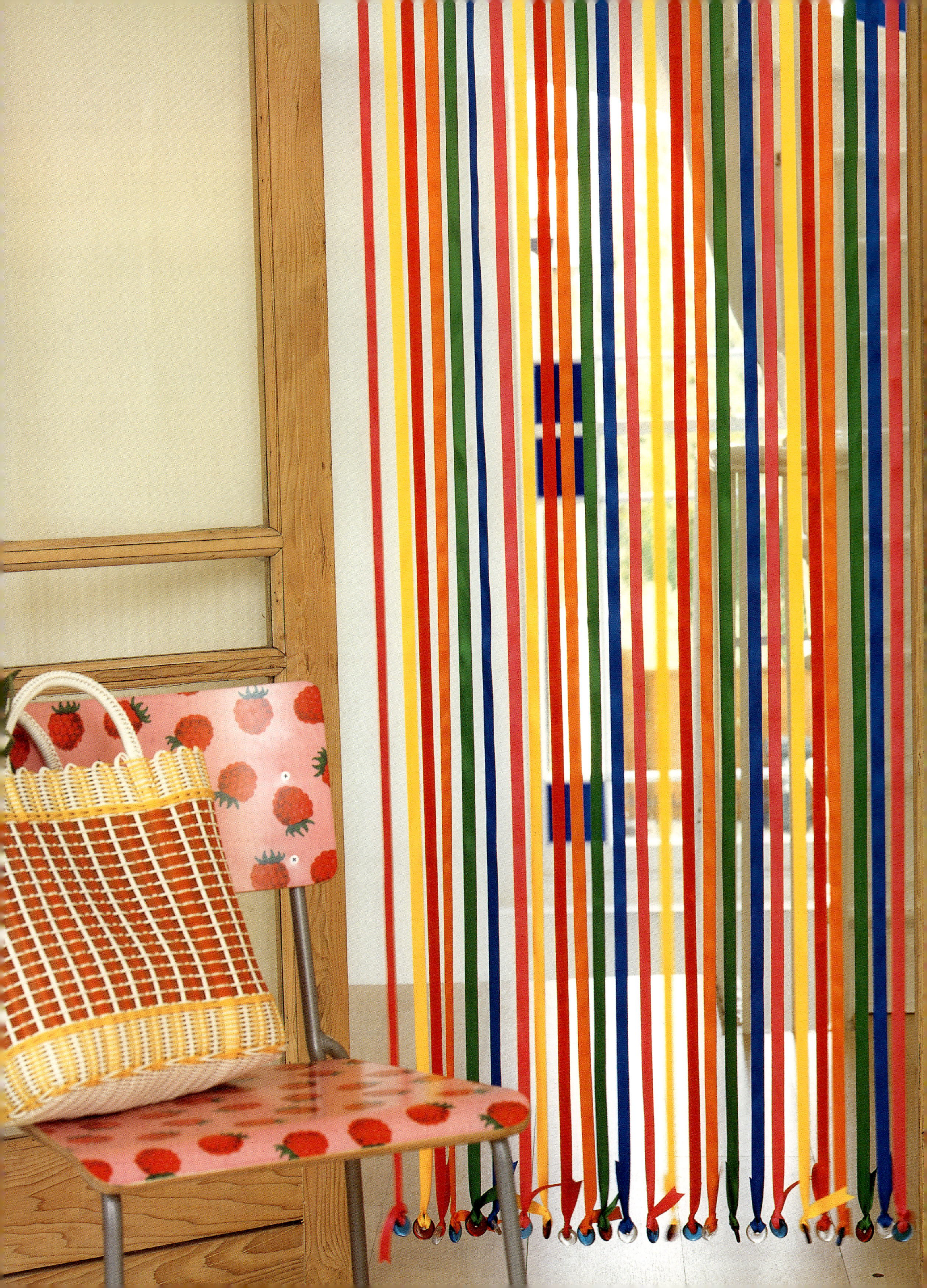

Golden Braid Cushion

Bring instant colour and a touch of Asian opulence to your home with this dazzling cushion. The richly textured woven metallic braids have a luxurious feel and many interesting combinations can be achieved.

you will need

Approximately 18 different patterned gold braids, 1m/40in of each

Red and green satin ribbons, 1.75m x 15mm/2yd x ⅝in

Tape measure

Scissors

Striped ticking, 75 x 40cm/30 x 16in

Dressmaker's pins

Needle and matching threads

Iron

Co-ordinating backing fabric, 60 x 30cm/24 x 12in

Cushion pad, 60 x 30cm/24 x 12in

Heavy gold furnishing cord, 1.75m/2yd

1 Cut the braids and ribbons into 40cm/16in lengths. Starting at the centre and using the woven lines of the ticking as a guide, pin the braid and ribbon in place. Arrange the colours for dramatic effect, interspersing the gold braid with red and green satin ribbons. Sew down using a narrow zigzag stitch, working slowly and carefully to avoid puckering.

2 When the ticking is completely covered, press from the back with a cool iron. Trim the edges so that the piece measures 60 x 30cm/24 x 12in. Turn under a 1cm/⅓in allowance on one short edge and hem. Make a 1cm/½in hem along one short edge of the backing fabric. With right sides facing, pin then sew the front and backing together around the three raw edges.

3 Clip the corners, turn through and press lightly. Insert the pad and slip stitch the opening (see Basic Stitching Techniques).

4 Slip stitch the furnishing cord around the edge of the cushion, making a small decorative loop at each corner.

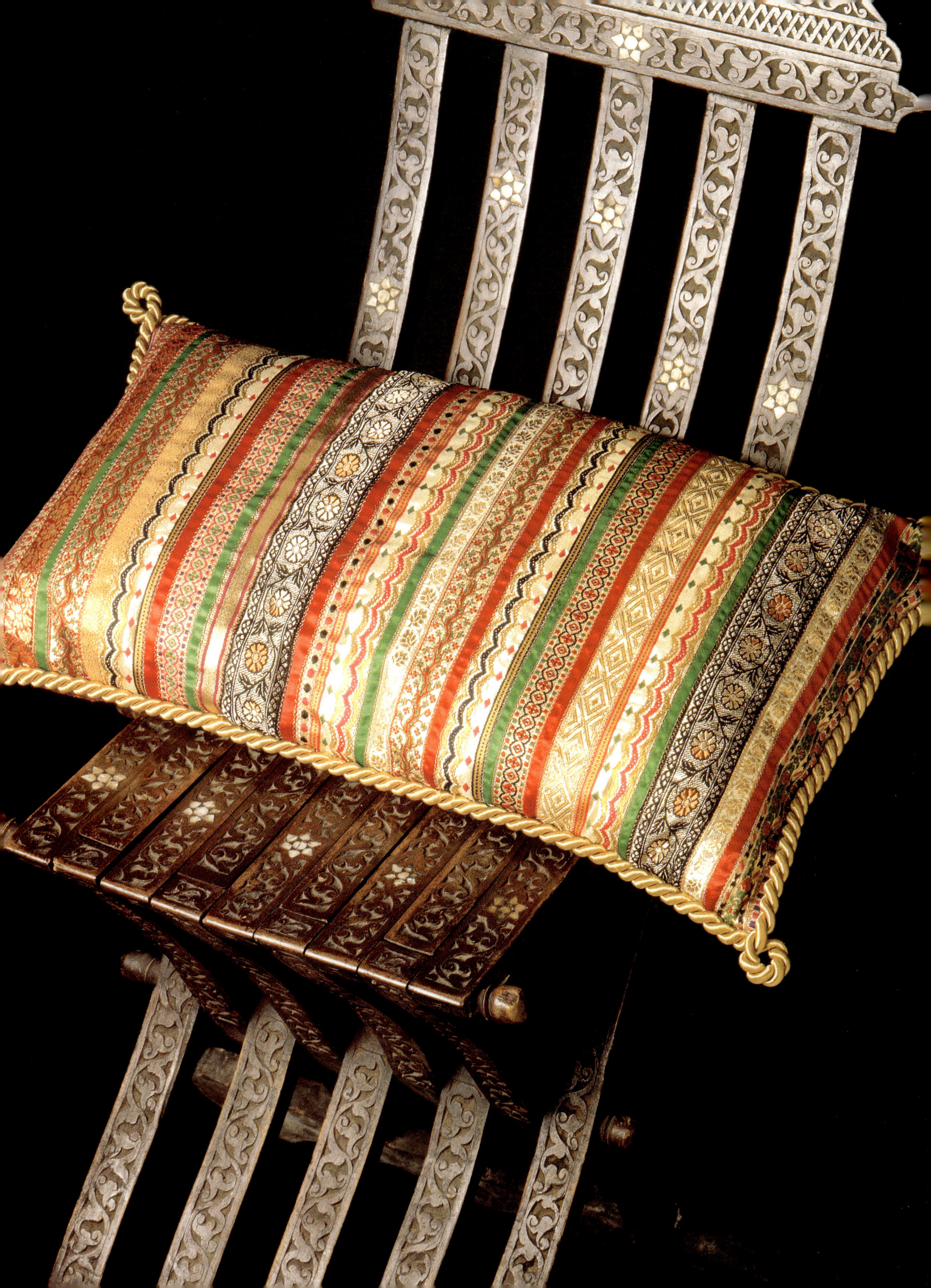

ribbonwork projects

A relatively small amount of expensive ribbon makes a big difference to this natural linen throw. Antique-style crushed velvet ribbon applied diagonally across the throw brings an element of real luxury.

Ribboned Throw

you will need
Natural linen, 1.5m/5ft square
Fabric marker
Ruler
Iron
Crushed velvet ribbons, 3cm/1¼in and 15mm/⅝in wide
Scissors
Dressmaker's pins
Tape measure
Sewing-machine
Matching thread
Silk lining, 167cm/5ft 7in square (widths joined if necessary)
Needle

1 Lay the linen flat, then use a ruler and fabric marker to mark a border all around the square, 7cm/2¾in from the edge. Fold two opposite corners together and press along the crease to make a diagonal fold across the centre.

2 Using the picture as a guide, pin the velvet ribbon diagonally across the linen following the direction of the fold and alternating the widths. Cut the ribbon to overlap the border by 2.5cm/1in at each end.

3 Machine stitch the ribbons in place, stitching close to the edges. To ensure that the ribbon lies flat, stitch both edges in the same direction.

4 With right sides together, match two opposite edges of the lining fabric to the border line marked on the linen. Pin and machine stitch the seams, starting and finishing 2cm/¾in from each end of the marked lines.

ribboned throw **49**

5 Match the two remaining edges in the same way. Machine stitch the edges together, leaving a 30cm/12in gap on one side.

6 Turn the fabric through to the right side. Centre the linen to give an even border 7cm/2¾in wide and press with a warm iron.

7 Turn in the lining along the opening edge and press. Slip stitch the gap closed. At the corners, trim and tuck in the excess fabric to form a mitred seam. Press and ladder stitch or slip stitch the folded edges together.

Striped Ribbon Cushion

Bands of satin, velvet and taffeta ribbon across this silk cushion make up a symphony of rich textures. Though all the tones are similar, light plays on the ribbons in different ways, creating dramatic contrasts.

you will need

Silk fabric, 80 x 45cm/32 x 18in
Tape measure
Dressmaking scissors
Iron
Selection of satin, velvet and taffeta ribbons
Dressmaker's pins
Needle and tacking (basting) thread
Stranded embroidery thread (floss) in complementary colours
Velvet, 20 x 40cm/8 x 16in
Sewing-machine, with zip foot
Matching thread
Piping cord, 2m/2yd
Zip, 40cm/16in
Cushion pad, 40cm/16in square

1 For the cushion front, cut a 45cm/18in square from the silk fabric. Fold diagonally through the centre and press. Arrange lengths of ribbon side by side across the fabric, using the fold as a guide, and pin in place. When you are satisfied with the ribbon positions, tack (baste) the ribbons to the front of the cushion.

2 Using stranded embroidery thread in a range of colours to complement the ribbons, work rows of feather stitch to join the edges, varying the direction of the stitches. Fold the velvet diagonally and cut 4cm/1½in wide strips parallel with the diagonal.

3 Stitch the short edges together with a 6mm/¼in seam allowance and press open to make a length of bias binding. Pin the binding around the piping cord and machine stitch in place.

4 Pin the covered cord all around the cushion front with the raw edges matching. Clip the seam allowance at the corners so that it lies flat. Tack, then machine stitch close to the cord.

striped ribbon cushion **51**

5 Unpick 2cm/¾in of the machine stitching from the beginning of the piping. Trim the cord so the ends butt together and lap one end of the casing over the other, turning under the raw edges. Pin to the cover and machine stitch. Slip stitch the casing edge.

6 For the cushion back, cut two pieces of silk 23 x 45cm/9 x 18in. With right sides together, match the two long edges and machine stitch using a long stitch setting. Press the seam open. Centre the zip over the back of the seam and tack in place.

7 Using a zip foot on the sewing-machine, top stitch around the zip. Unpick the temporary seam. Undo the zip. With right sides together, pin and machine stitch the cushion back and front together, following the line of piping. Clip the corners, turn through and insert the cushion pad.

Sunflower-motif Jacket

Customize a child's denim jacket with this colourful sunflower. Ribbon appliqué is deceptively simple to work, as the woven edges mean no fussy hemming, and tricky curves and angles are easy.

you will need
Denim jacket
Brown double-face satin ribbon, 1.5m x 1cm/1⅔yd x ½in
Needle and matching threads
Yellow double-face satin ribbon, 1m x 4cm/40 x 1½in
Scissors
Leaf-green double-face satin ribbon, 50 x 4cm/40 x 1½in
Embroidery threads (floss)

1 Mark the design area on the jacket as a rough guide for the appliqué work. Start by stitching the end of the brown ribbon to the centre of the design area. Sew the ribbon in a spiral, overlapping the coils and turning the ribbon over itself to form a circle. Sew along the inside edge of the ribbon as you make the spiral, using back stitch or running stitch to secure the outer edge of the previous coil (see Basic Techniques). Leave the outer edge of the completed spiral unsewn.

2 Make 11 flower petal shapes from yellow ribbon, snipping a curve along each side of the tip without cutting the straight edges.

3 Stitch the petals around the flower centre, turning under the raw edges and tucking the base of each petal under the unsewn edge of the centre of the flower.

4 Continue adding petals around the centre, overlapping some of the edges. Leave a gap at the bottom for the last two flower petals to be added after the flower stem.

sunflower-motif jacket **53**

5 Cut the flower stem from the leaf-green ribbon. Tuck one end under the outer edge of the flower centre and sew the stem in place, using green embroidery thread. Turn under the bottom raw edge before stitching. Sew the last two petals over the stem.

6 Sew down the outer edge of the flower centre, securing the petals and the top of the stem. Decorate the centre with French knots of various sizes worked in brown embroidery thread.

7 To finish off, cut two leaves from the green ribbon and stitch to either side of the stem. Stitch veins on the leaves using a small running stitch and green embroidery thread.

Ribbon Jewellery

A great advantage of ribbon is its versatility. Here pieces of richly patterned ribbon have been fashioned into a stunning necklace – an idea that could be extended to make a bracelet or earrings to match.

you will need
Thin white card (stock)
Pencil
Ruler
Scissors
Wire-edged patterned ribbon, 40 x 5cm/16 x 2in
Super epoxy clear glue
Glue spreader or paintbrush
Needle and matching thread
Round and tubular beads, 15mm/⅝in wide
Plastic-coated garden wire
Toning ribbon, approximately 75cm x 3mm/30 x ⅛in
Small gold beads
Necklace clasp

1 Cut six 7 x 4cm/2¾ x 1½in rectangles from the card and roll each one carefully into a tube.

2 Cut six 7cm/2¾in strips of patterned ribbon, selecting the pattern area you want to use along the ribbon. Glue one end of each piece of ribbon on to the outside end of each tube of paper. Allow to dry.

3 Fold over the other end of the ribbon by 6mm/¼in. Roll the ribbon around the tube so that the edges of the ribbon meet. Stitch down the join. Push the wired edges of the ribbon into the tube. Apply glue to both ends of the tubes and press on a bead.

4 Hold the beads in place while the glue dries by threading a piece of wire through each tube and bending the end around. Thread the ribbon-covered tubes on to the 3mm/⅛in ribbon with gold and coloured beads arranged in a repeating pattern in between.

5 Thread a clasp on to the ends of the ribbon. Fold each ribbon end back on itself and stitch down, wrapping the thread over the stitching. Knot the end of the ribbon and wrap again with thread to cover the knot. Secure the thread firmly before cutting it off.

ribbon jewellery 55

Tartan Ribbon Roses

Fun to make and bound to be a conversation piece, these plaid roses can be adapted to suit many festive occasions: as part of a garland, as a table centrepiece or stitched to a bag, gown or satin slippers.

you will need

For one rose:

Tartan ribbon, 60 x 4cm/24 x 1½in
Stub (floral) wire, 20cm/8in
Needle and matching thread
Craft scissors
Tartan wire-edged ribbon, 30 x 4cm/12 x 1½in
Fine florist's wire
Florist's tape (stem wrap)

1 Bend the end of a piece of stub wire to form a hook equal in depth to the ribbon width. Holding the tartan ribbon with the cut end to the right, hook the wire through the upper right-hand corner of the ribbon, approximately 6mm/¼in from the edge. Close the hook to hold the ribbon in place.

2 Roll the ribbon around the hook two or three times from right to left to enclose the wire. Stitch at the base to secure. Then, holding the wire stem in your right hand and the loose ribbon in your left, fold the ribbon so that it runs downwards, parallel to the wire.

3 Roll the covered hook end from right to left into the fold, turning tightly at the bottom and loosely at the top until the ribbon is once again horizontal to the wire.

4 With the wire stem facing towards you, stitch the base of the rose to secure the petal in place.

5 Continue folding the ribbon and rolling the rose in this way, stitching the base after each fold until you have the desired shape and size of rose. To complete the rose, cut the ribbon squarely, fold it back on to the rose and stitch in place.

tartan ribbon roses **57**

6 To make a leaf, cut the wire-edged ribbon into 10cm/4in lengths. Cut three 20cm/8in lengths of florist's wire and make a small loop 2.5cm/1in from the end of each one. Fold two corners of a piece of ribbon down and forward into a triangle. Place a wire in the centre with the short end upwards and stitch it in place.

7 Fold the lower corners of the ribbon triangle under and backwards to create a leaf shape. Gather the lower part of the leaf neatly around the long wire stem and stitch to secure in place. Make two more leaves in this way.

8 Bind the wire stems of two leaves with florist's tape for 1cm/½in. Bind the wire stem of the third leaf for 2.5cm/1in. Join the three leaves together at this point and continue binding all three wires to create a single stem. Bind the rose stem, adding in the triple leaf about 10cm/4in down from the flower.

58 ribbonwork projects

Lantern frames are available in many different shapes and sizes, so this idea is very versatile. Measure the four sides of the frame and select a width of ribbon that can be multiplied to fit into this length exactly.

Ribbon Lantern

you will need
Basic lantern frame
Tape measure
Ribbon, length and width depending on size of frame
Scissors
Iron
Needle and matching threads
Beads (one small, one large and one rocaille per ribbon)
PVA (white) glue

1 Cut pieces of ribbon to twice the finished frame length. To mitre one end of each ribbon, turn in 1cm/½in along the raw edge and press lightly with a dry iron to hold in place.

2 Fold in one corner to the centre of the ribbon, then fold in the other corner to make a triangular, mitred point. Iron to hold in position.

3 Thread a needle and tie a knot in one end. Pass the needle through the point of the mitre, then thread a small bead followed by a large bead and a rocaille. Pass the needle back through the large and small bead so the rocaille forms a stopper. Secure with a small stitch on the inside of the point.

4 Starting close to the final stitch, slip stitch along the central join of the mitre, keeping a neat point at the end of the triangle (see Basic Techniques).

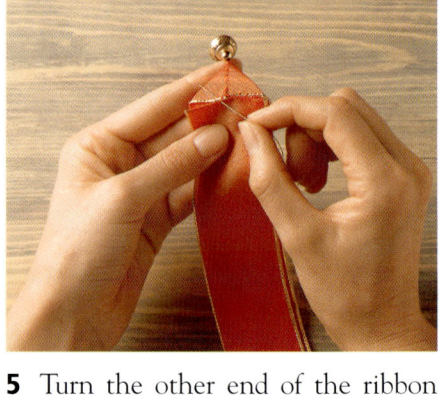

5 Turn the other end of the ribbon over, and loop the ribbon over one side of the frame. Fold under and slip stitch the other end of the ribbon to the top of the mitre, making sure that the wrong sides of the ribbon will be inside the frame. Make all the other ribbons in this way.

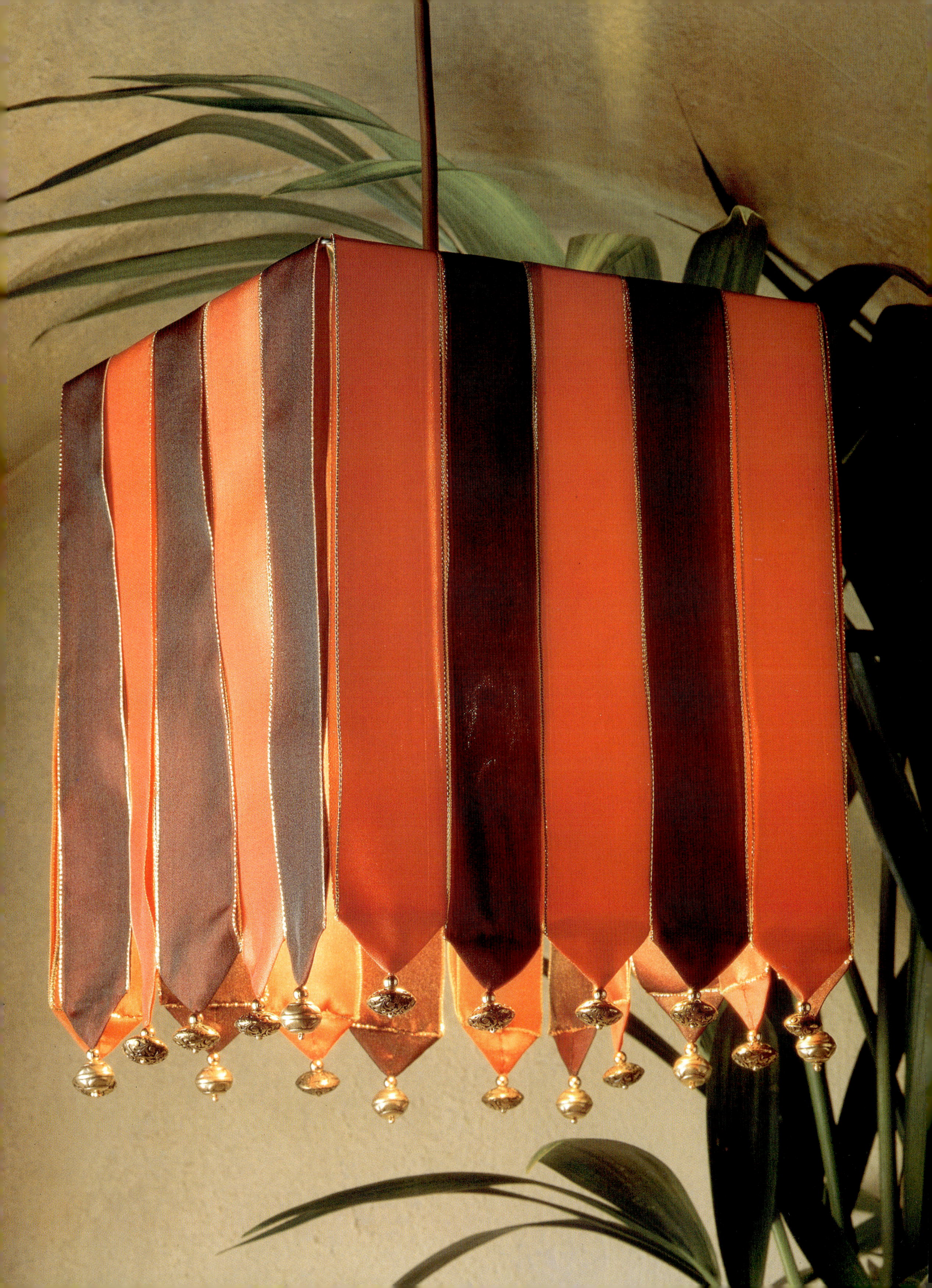

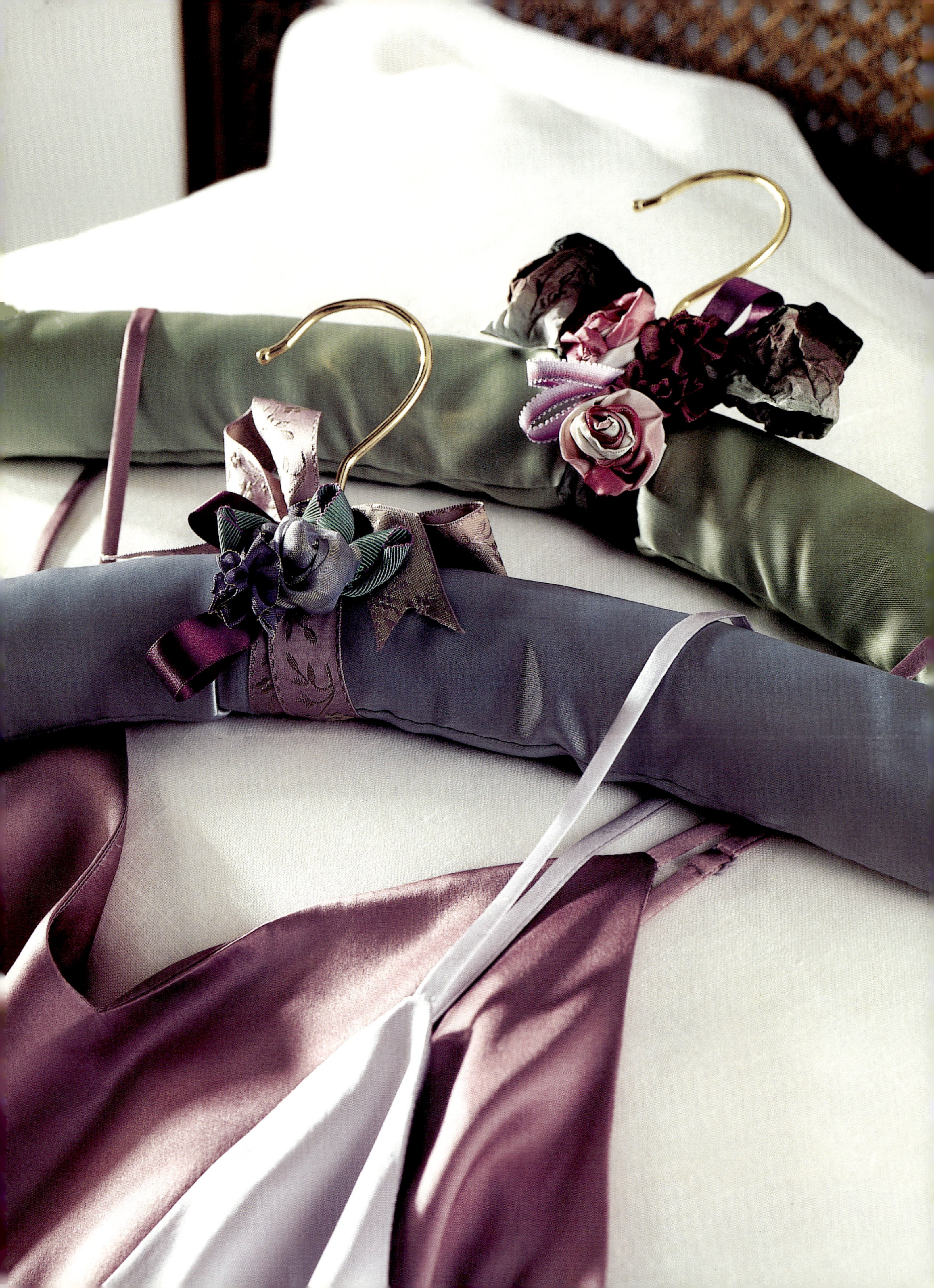

Ribbon-Rose Coat Hangers

Give your prettiest clothes the care they deserve with these luxurious padded hangers, decorated with roses and bows made from exquisite silk and brocade ribbons in beautiful muted shades.

you will need
Polyester wadding (batting)
Scissors
Wooden coat hangers
Needle and matching thread
Satin ribbon, 8cm/3in wide
Selection of organza, silk, petersham or grosgrain and brocade ribbons

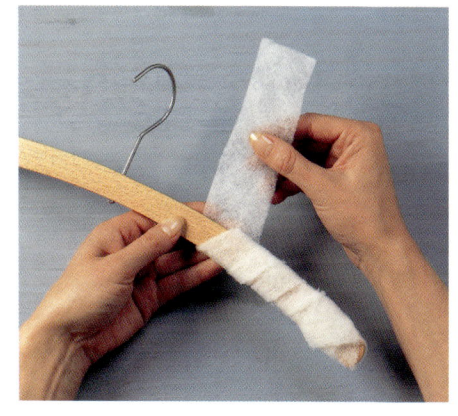

1 Cut a 5cm/2in wide strip of polyester wadding and wind it around the wooden part of a hanger. Secure it with a few stitches at each end.

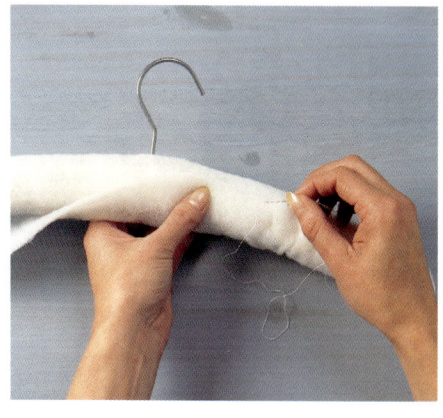

2 Cut a long, narrow rectangle of wadding to cover the hanger. Fold it over the bound wadding and sew in place along the top edge, folding over and neatening the ends as you go.

3 Cut two lengths of wide satin ribbon to make the cover for the hanger and, with right sides together, stitch each end in a gentle curve.

4 Stitch the two ribbons together along one long edge of the satin cover and turn to the right side.

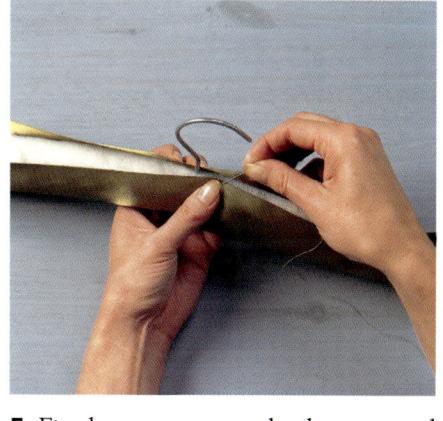

5 Fit the cover over the hanger and slip stitch the top edges neatly, gathering the ends gently and easing in the fullness as you sew.

62 ribbonwork projects

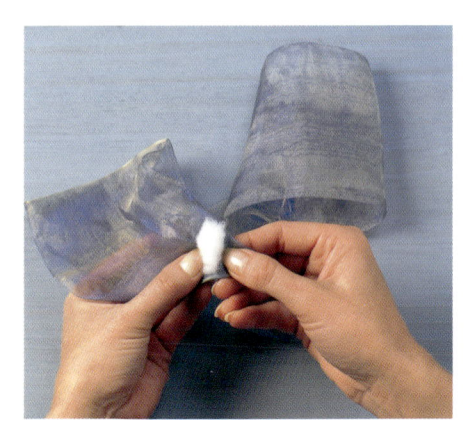

6 To make a rose to decorate the hanger, fold a tiny piece of wadding into the end of a length of organza ribbon and secure with a stitch.

7 Fold and wind the rest of the ribbon around this central bud, stitching through the layers to secure. Tuck in the raw edge and stitch down. Make two roses for each hanger.

8 To make a rosette, cut a length of silk ribbon about five times its width and join the raw edges.

9 Gather the ribbon with a running stitch slightly above the centre. Pull up and secure. Flatten the ribbon out with your fingers to complete the rosette. Make two for each hanger.

10 To make a leaf, take a small piece of green petersham or grosgrain ribbon and fold both ends down to the side. Work a running stitch along this side and pull up the gathers tightly, securing with a stitch. Make four for each hanger.

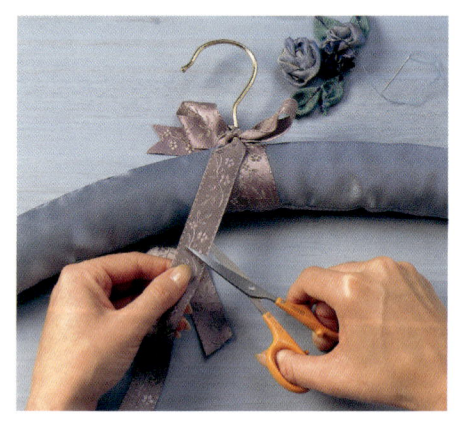

11 Tie a length of brocade ribbon around the centre of each hanger to finish in a bow around the hook. Use this as a foundation to attach the roses, leaves and rosettes. Decorate with loops of ribbon to make a pleasing arrangement.

Hat boxes make ideal storage containers for all sorts of items beside hats. The basic boxes can be bought from stationery or gift shops and, with a little imagination, the decorative possibilities are endless.

Ribbon Hat Box

you will need

35cm/14in diameter hat box
Patterned fabric, 1.5m x 115cm/1⅔yd x 45in
Dressmaking scissors
Iron
Glue gun or contact adhesive
Heavy gold cord, 1.75m/2yd
Thin card (stock)
Lining fabric, 40 x 90cm/16 x 36in
Polyester wadding (batting), 38 x 75cm/15 x 30in
Matching sewing thread
Plain ribbon, 1m x 10cm/1yd x 4in
Wire-edged gilded ribbon, 1.8m x 10cm/2yd x 4in
3 bunches artificial grapes
2 gold tassels

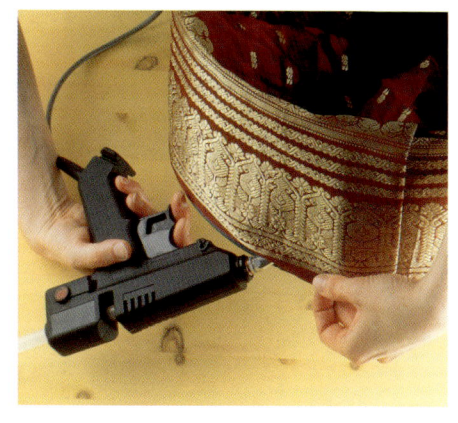

1 Cut a length of patterned fabric slightly longer than the circumference of the box and 2½ times its height. Press under 1cm/½in along one short side, then glue the fabric to the box using a glue gun or impact adhesive. Overlap the folded edge to make a neat join.

2 With the point of a pair of scissors, make a small hole ⅔ of the way up each side. Cut a 75cm/30in length of gold cord, and insert through the holes to form a carrying handle. Knot securely on the inside and glue in position if necessary.

3 Cut a circle from card measuring 1cm/½in less in diameter than the base of the box. Cut out a slightly larger circle of lining fabric and use it to cover one side of the card. Smooth the fabric to prevent any wrinkles forming, then turn over and glue down the edges.

4 Fold the excess patterned fabric into the box to line the inside, smoothing the fabric so it lies neatly. Stick the covered circle to the base of the box, with the fabric-covered side uppermost. Any surplus lining fabric will be hidden underneath the card circle.

▶

5 Cut a circle of wadding to fit the top of the box lid and glue in place. Cut a circle of the remaining fabric, slightly larger than the radius and circumference of the box lid. Glue this around the outside of the lid, matching the edge of the material with the edge of the lid to leave excess for gathering.

6 Run a gathering thread through the fabric 18cm/7in from the rim, draw up and secure.

7 Cut the plain ribbon in half and stretch one piece across the lid, gluing the ends inside the rim. Knot the other piece to the centre and glue the ends inside the rim, at right angles to the first.

8 Glue gold cord around the outside of the rim. Butt the two ends together and cover with a narrow strip of fabric to neaten the join.

9 Make a bow from the wire-edged ribbon. Cut the ends in fishtails and shape the loops. Glue to the centre of the lid, then stick on the grapes.

10 Finish off by sewing a tassel to each end of the handle.

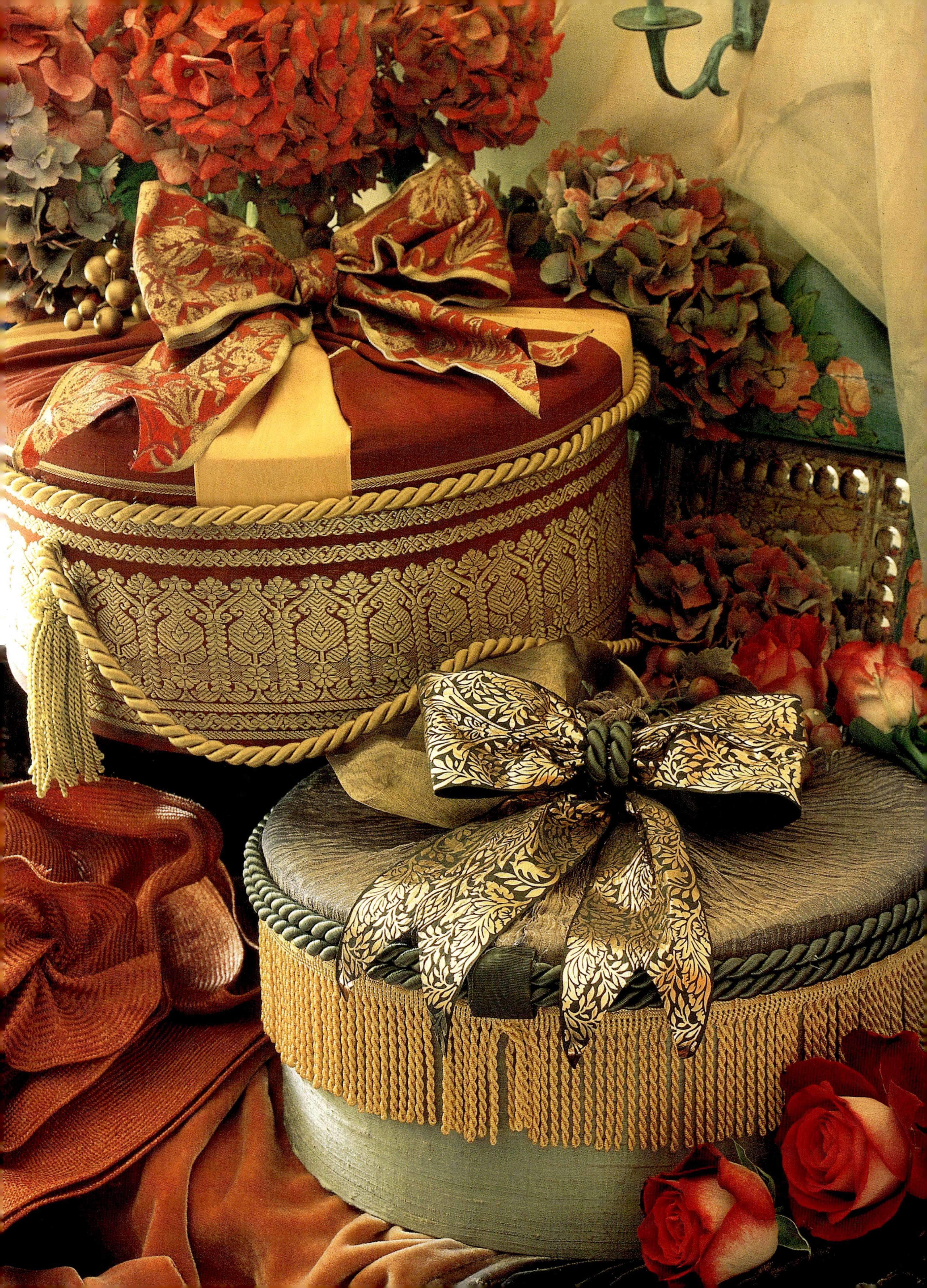

ribbonwork projects

The cover for this striped lampshade consists entirely of ribbons, allowing you to introduce a rich variety of colour and texture. They are simply stuck side by side on to a piece of lampshade backing material.

Satin and Velvet Ribbon Shade

you will need
Graph paper
Pencil
Drum-shaped lampshade frame with reversible gimbal, top diameter 18cm/7in, bottom diameter 20cm/8in, height 20cm/8in
Scissors
Self-adhesive lampshade backing material
Satin bias binding
Selection of coloured velvet and satin ribbons
White (PVA) glue
Clothes pegs (pins)
Needle
Matching thread
Ceramic lamp base
Spray enamel paint and face mask

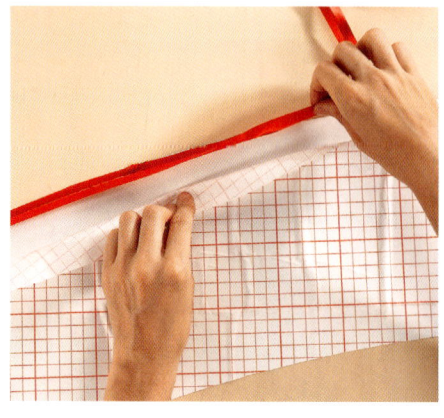

1 Make a paper pattern to fit the frame. Cut a piece of self-adhesive backing material to the size of the pattern. Remove the backing paper from the lower edge of the backing material to expose the adhesive. Cut a piece of satin bias binding to the length of the lower edge plus 2cm/¾in. Press one edge of the bias binding to the lower edge of the backing material.

2 Cut lengths of satin and velvet ribbon to fit the circumference of the shade, leaving a 1cm/½in overlap at one end. Lay a length of ribbon alongside the bias binding, following the curve of the pattern. Lay more lengths of ribbon across the backing until the last one is 6mm/¼in from the top edge. Alternate velvet with different coloured satin, and remove the paper.

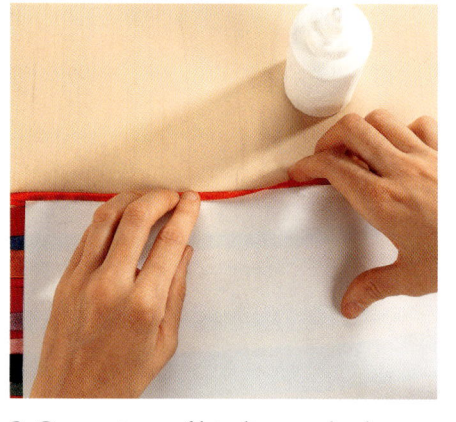

3 Cut a piece of binding to fit the top edge, with a 2cm/¾in allowance. Lay one edge of the bias binding along the top edge. Apply glue to the wrong side of the backing at top and bottom. Fold over to the wrong side.

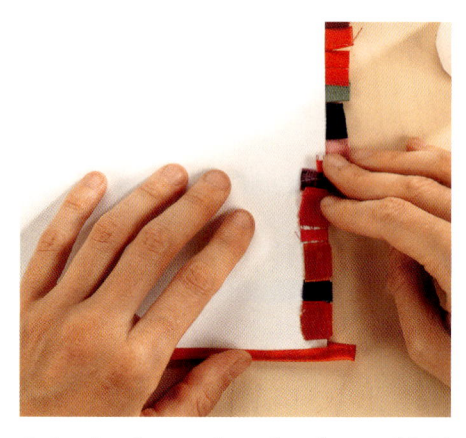

4 Apply glue to the side edge and fold the raw ribbon ends to the wrong side. Leave to dry. If the ribbons begin to curl away from the backing, place under a heavy object. Neaten untidy edges or hanging threads with scissors.

satin and velvet ribbon shade **67**

5 Apply a thin line of glue to the underside of the same edge. Take care to wipe away any glue that squeezes on to the ribbons. Roll into a drum shape and lap the glued edge over the opposite edge, matching up the stripes of colours perfectly. Use two clothes pegs to hold the edges together firmly at the top and bottom until the glue is completely dry.

6 Where the raw edges of the bias binding meet, turn under 1cm/½in of one raw edge and stick it down so that it overlaps the other raw edge. Use the clothes pegs to hold the bindings together until the glue is dry. Slip stitch the folded edge in place. Apply a line of glue to the outside edge of the frame and insert it into the cover.

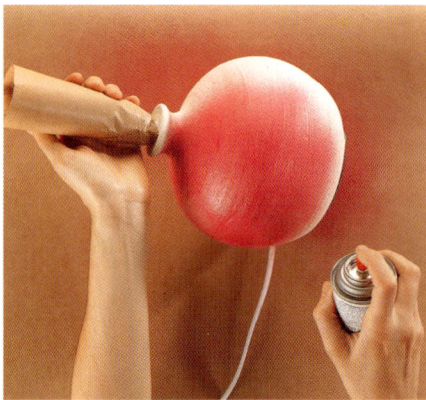

7 Working in a well-ventilated space, and wearing a face mask, spray the lamp base with a thin coat of pink enamel paint. Leave to dry before applying a second coat. Spray the shade with flame retarder if necessary, before attaching to the base. Use a medium-wattage bulb.

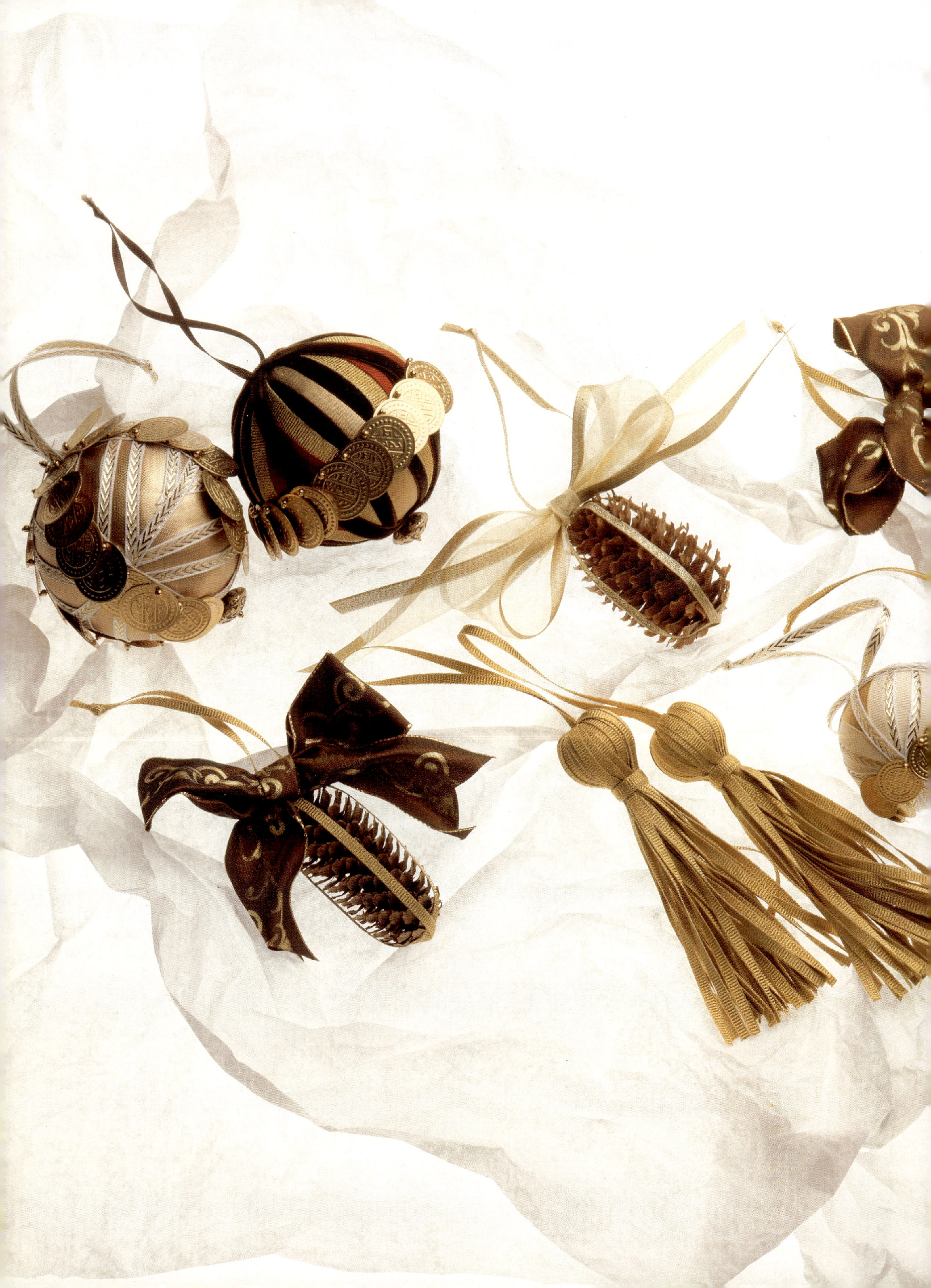

These subtle ribbon decorations – a combination of earthy colours and natural textures – make a welcome change from glitzy baubles. Hang them from a tree or wreath, or string them along the mantelpiece.

Ribbon Christmas Decorations

you will need
Baubles:
Polystyrene (styrofoam) balls, 7.5 or 5cm/3 or 2in diameter
Pencil
Tape measure
Gold, brown and cream ribbons, 1m x 3–9mm/40in x 1/8–3/8in
Dressmaker's pins
Scissors
Toning patterned ribbon, 2m x 3–10mm/2 1/4yd x 1/8–1/2in
Tiny gold beads
Gold-coin pendants
Brass lace pins
Large, ornate gold beads

Pine cone parcels:
Gold, lemon or brown ribbon, 4cm/1 1/2in wide
Gold or brown ribbon, 3mm/1/8in wide
Pine cones
White (PVA) glue

Golden tassel:
Cotton-pulp ball, 2.5cm/1in in diameter
Scissors
Gold grosgrain ribbon, 10m x 3mm/11yd x 1/8in
Crewel needle
White (PVA) glue

Baubles

1 Draw lines on a polystyrene ball to divide it vertically into four segments, then mark horizontally round the sphere to divide it into eighths. Place a length of ribbon along one quarter, pin the ends on the lines and trim. Fill in the section with a patchwork of assorted ribbons, taking care to overlap the edges.

2 Fill in each section. Lay the patterned ribbon over the pins and ribbon ends, following the guidelines, and pin at each point where the lines cross. Fold under the ends to neaten. Make a hanging loop by slipping a 25cm/10in length of ribbon under one intersection and knotting the ends.

3 Slip a tiny gold bead and a coin pendant on to each of 15 brass lace pins. Pin them in a row around the centre. Thread a small and a large bead on to the last pin and stick into the base of the ball to complete. Make other baubles in the same way, using different ribbons.

Pine cone parcels

Tie the wide ribbon into a bow (see Basic Techniques). Wrap the narrow ribbon around a pine cone, as if wrapping a parcel, tying off at the tip. Dab with glue to secure. Make a hanging loop by tying the ends together 10cm/4in from the knot. Glue the bow to the top of the cone.

Golden tassel

1 Use scissors to make a hole through the centre of the cotton-pulp ball. Pull out some of the fibre to enlarge the hole to 1cm/½in in diameter. Cut 25cm/10in grosgrain ribbon, then cut the rest into 30cm/12in lengths.

2 Put the 25cm/10in and a 30cm/12in length aside and use the crewel needle to thread the others through the hole. Allow 12.5cm/5in of each ribbon to hang below the ball. Spread glue thinly over the ball. Fold down the ribbons protruding from the top to cover the ball completely.

3 Thread the needle with the 25cm/10in length of ribbon. Glue one end around the ribbons close to the base of the ball. Wrap the ribbon tightly around the tassel.

4 Insert the needle behind the binding ribbon and pull tightly. Unthread the needle, allowing the ribbon end to hang down with the other ribbons. Do not trim at this stage.

5 To suspend the tassel, double the 30cm/12in length of ribbon and thread it through the needle. Insert the needle down through the hole in the ball. Remove the needle, knot the ends neatly together and trim. Gently pull the loop taut, hiding the knot among the ribbons. Trim the ends.

Ruched organza ribbons, sewn on to translucent voile in a fine tracery of delicate spirals, give an interesting, three-dimensional effect to this light and airy curtain.

Appliquéd Ribbon Café Curtain

you will need
Tape measure
Voile
Dressmaking scissors
Dressmaker's pins
Sewing-machine
Matching thread
Iron
Thin card (stock)
Pencil
Fabric marker
Needle
Organza ribbons in green and pink

1 Calculate the width and drop of the curtain and cut out the voile, adding 5cm/2in to the width and 15cm/6in to the length. To make the facing, cut a second piece of voile to the same width by 30cm/12in. Turn under and machine stitch a 6mm/¼in hem along the lower edge of the facing. Press. With right sides together, pin the facing to the curtain, matching the top edges.

2 Enlarge the scallop template at the back of the book, and cut out of thin card. Add the width of the template to the proposed width of each fabric loop (4–7cm/1½–2¾in) and divide the finished curtain width by this figure to calculate the number of scallops required. Allow for a strip at each end of the curtain. Draw around the template along the top of the curtain, using a fabric marker.

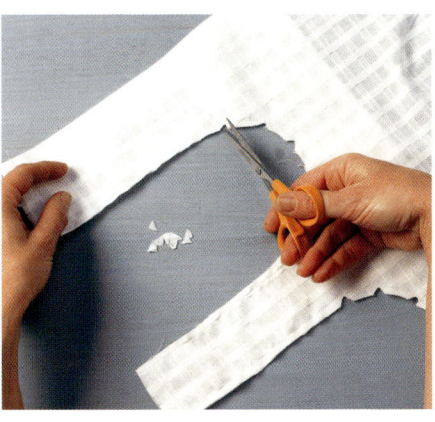

3 Machine stitch the facing to the curtain along the marked lines. Cut out the scallops, leaving a 1cm/½in seam allowance. Clip the corners and snip into the curves.

4 Turn the curtain through to the right side and press. Topstitch around the seams, 4mm/⅕in from the edge.

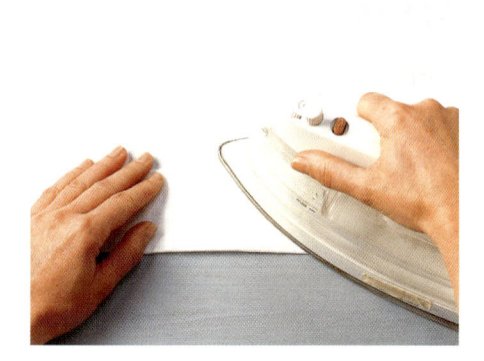

5 Turn under and press a double hem 1cm/½in wide down each side edge of the curtain. Turn under and press a 5cm/2in double hem along the bottom edge.

6 Mitre the corners and slip stitch them neatly in place. Turn under and press a 1cm/½in single hem down both side edges of the facing. Slip stitch the facing and all the hems in place.

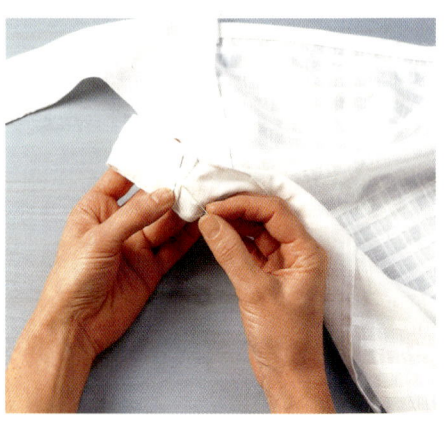

7 To make the fabric hanging loops, turn 5cm/2in of each strip to the wrong side of the curtain. Pin and slip stitch them to the facing, taking care not to let the needle pass through to the right side.

8 Cut the green ribbon into 1m/1yd lengths. Set the machine to a long straight stitch and sew down the centre of each length. Pull up the bobbin thread from each end to gather the ribbon, then adjust the ruffles so that they lie evenly.

9 Draw a series of freehand spirals randomly across the curtain, using a fabric marker. Pin the ruched ribbons along the lines. Machine stitch along the gathering threads, being careful not to trap the ribbon under the stitches.

10 Gather the pink ribbon as before and cut a strip 15cm/6in long for each flower. Fold each one into three small loops and pin the flowers to the curtain in the spaces between the spirals. Machine stitch, securing the loops in place. Insert a narrow pole through the hanging loops and fix it in place at the window.

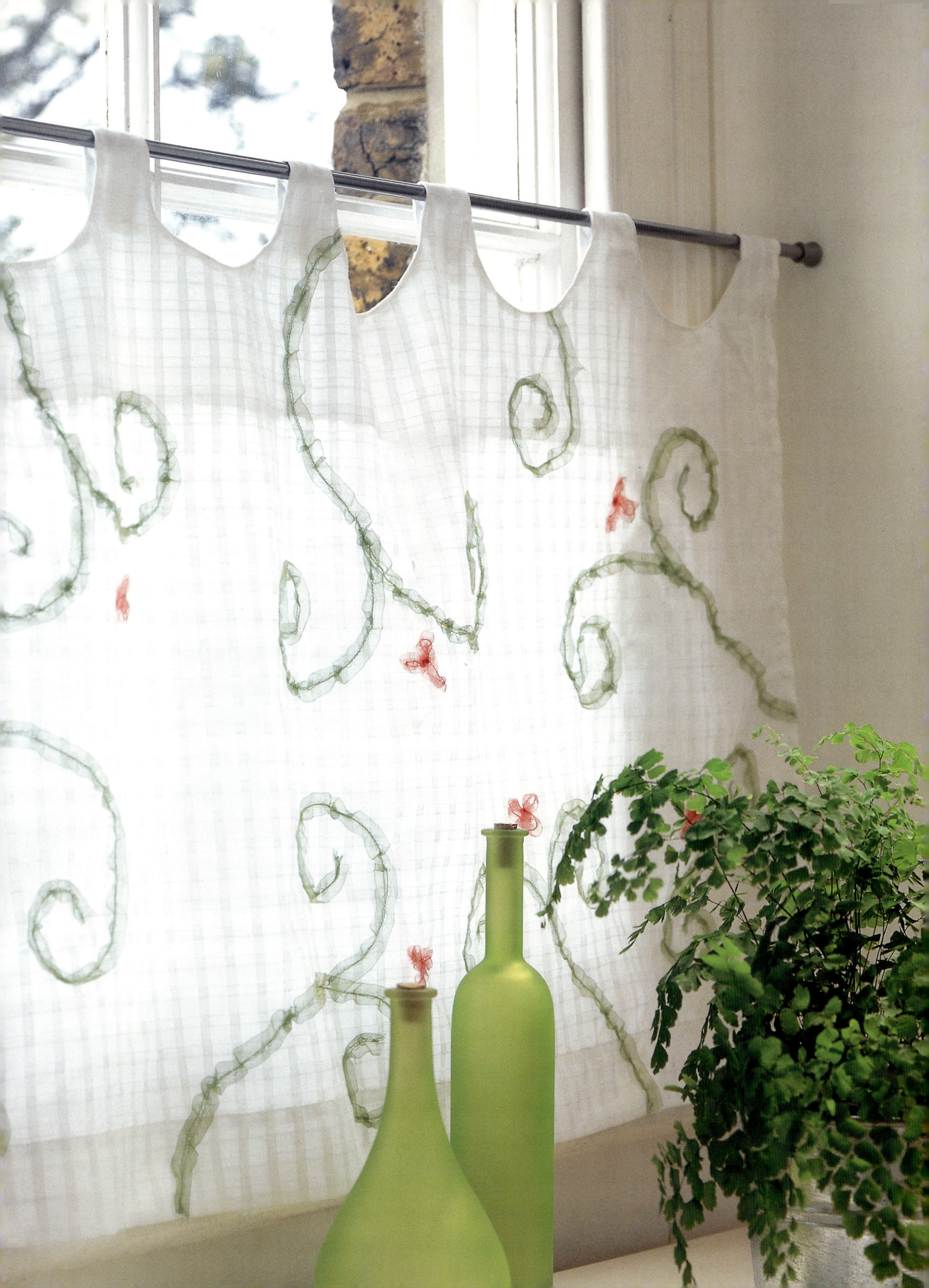

Deck-chair Cover

An old deckchair can be transformed with a new cover and an interesting way to make this is with grosgrain ribbon. Here, two contrasting colours have been interwoven to make a chequerboard effect.

you will need
Deckchair
Claw hammer or pliers
medium-grade abrasive paper
Large sheet of card (stock)
Tape measure
Pencil
Grosgrain ribbon in white and blue, 4cm/1½in wide (10m/11yd is sufficient for a small chair)
Scissors
Drawing pins (thumb tacks)
Dressmaker's pins
Needle and tacking (basting) thread
Sewing-machine and matching thread
Staple gun

1 Remove the existing canvas from the chair frame, setting it aside to use as a template and carefully prising out any old fabric fixings with a claw hammer or pliers. Sand down any rough edges on the frame and repaint if necessary.

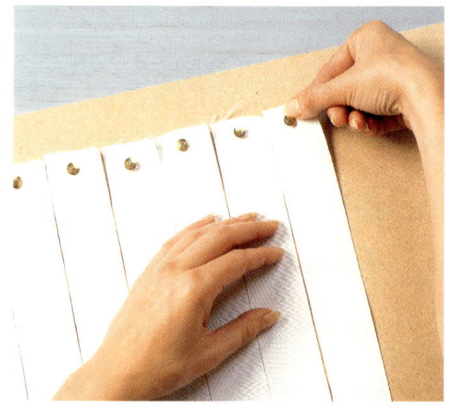

2 Mark the dimensions of the cover on the sheet of cardboard. Cut lengths of white grosgrain ribbon to the length of the measured rectangle, plus about 10cm/4in for fixing. Pin the ribbons to the board side by side along the top of the rectangle to form the "warp".

3 Cut lengths of blue ribbon to fit across the rectangle and form the "weft". To weave the cover, pin a blue ribbon to the warp length at one side, weave it under and over the warp until you reach the other side, then pin securely again.

4 Continue weaving until you have the size required. When complete, tack (baste) across the edges of the woven piece to hold the warp in place. Cut two lengths of blue ribbon to fit down each side of the new cover. Lay one length over the raw edges of the weft at each side and tack in position.

5 Remove the cover from the board and machine-stitch the blue and white ribbons together, stitching very close to both edges. Attach the new cover to the wooden frame by wrapping the ends of the ribbons around the horizontal rungs and stapling them securely in place.

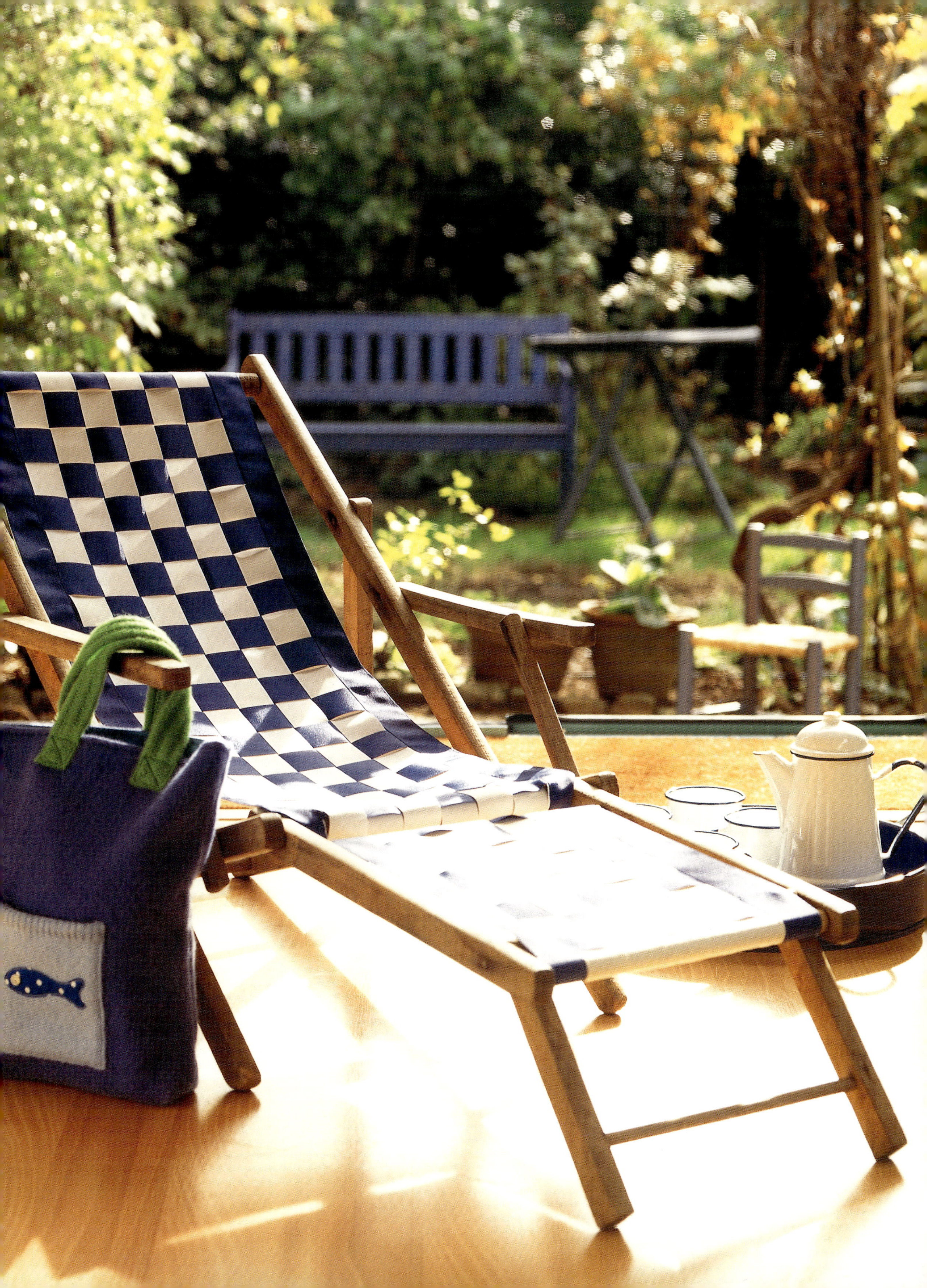

The openweave effect used to make this plush cover allows the dark blue moiré taffeta backing fabric to show through the complementing richness of the brocade, velvet and jacquard ribbons.

Basket-weave Cushion

you will need
Dark blue moiré taffeta, 1m x 38cm/1yd x 15in
Dressmaking scissors
Ruler
Black rosebud brocade ribbon, 1.15m x 2cm/1¼yd x ¾in
Claret rosebud brocade ribbon, 1.15m x 2cm/1¼yd x ¾in
Dressmaker's pins
Claret velvet ribbon, 1.15m x 23mm/1¼yd x ⅞in
Purple marble-print ribbon, 1.15m x 23mm/1¼yd x ⅞in
Dark red ribbon, 1.15m x 25mm/1¼yd x 1in
Claret jacquard ribbon, 1.15m x 7mm/1¼yd x ⅜in
Green velvet ribbon, 2.5m x 2cm/2¾yd x ¾in
Needle and matching threads
Iron and pressing cloth
Cushion pad, 36cm/14in square

1 Fold a 35cm/14in square of taffeta into quarters. Cut all the ribbons into 35cm/14 in lengths. Lay a brocade ribbon along each crease, then put a velvet ribbon 3mm/⅛in away from each side of the cross. Interweave the ribbons, pinning them down at the ends and the crossing points.

2 Using a ruler to ensure that all the lines are straight, continue to weave in the other ribbons, following the design of the completed cushion. When the weave is complete, pin all the loose ribbon ends to the backing fabric.

3 Starting at one edge, sew the ribbons to the taffeta by making two small, neat overstitches across each point where the ribbons overlap. Sew the ribbons firmly in place but avoid pulling the thread too tightly across the back, as this will distort the weave.

4 Cut two 35 x 25cm/14 x 10in taffeta rectangles. Hem one long side of each. Right sides facing, pin to the cushion front so the hems overlap in the centre and the cut edges match. Stitch all round 2cm/¾in from the edge. Clip the corners, turn through, press and insert the cushion pad.

basket-weave cushion **77**

Ribbon is ideal for weaving, and wonderful effects can be achieved with subtle combinations of colour and texture. This headboard sets the tone for a minimalist bedroom in neutral shades.

Woven Ribbon Headboard

you will need

Length of 25 x 25mm/1 x 1in wooden batten (furring strip)
Hacksaw
medium-grade abrasive paper
Drill and bit
Tape measure
Pencil
Wood glue
Dowels
4 right-angled fixing brackets
Screws
Screwdriver
Grosgrain ribbon in blue, brown and beige, 5m x 12mm/5½yd x ½in
Cream satin or taffeta ribbon, 20m x 2.5cm/22yd x 1in
Satin striped ribbon in blue, brown and beige, 5m x 3cm/5½yd x 1¼in
Grosgrain ribbon in blue, brown and beige, 5m x 15mm 5½yd x ⅝in
Scissors
Staple gun

1 Using the hacksaw, cut the softwood batten into four lengths, each measuring 90cm/36in. This will make a headboard to fit a single bed: increase the width of the board for a larger bed and increase the amount of ribbon proportionately. Sand the cut edges.

2 Use a drill with a bit to fit the dowels to make a hole at each end of the two battens that will form the horizontal pieces of the frame. Drill a hole 1cm/½in from the top of each side piece and a second hole 60cm/24in down. Glue the dowel joints and assemble the frame.

3 Screw four right-angled fixing brackets to the reverse side of the headboard frame to reinforce the joints and hold the frame rigid while you work. This will help to keep the woven pattern symmetrical.

4 Cut the ribbons into 70cm/28in lengths. Lay them vertically on the frame in a symmetrical pattern: start at the centre with a wide grosgrain overlaid with a light satin striped ribbon, then work outwards with alternate narrower satin and grosgrain ribbon.

woven ribbon headboard **79**

5 Repeat the sequence to fill the frame. Staple the ribbons to the frame, pulling each piece taut. Cut two short pieces of cream satin or taffeta ribbon and staple to cover the wooden batten at the top two corners.

6 Interweave ribbons horizontally across the headboard in a pattern sequence similar to the warp. Turn the headboard over and staple the raw ends securely to the frame as before, making sure that the ribbons are pulled quite taut.

80 ribbonwork projects

Join lengths of Fortuny-style pleated ribbon to make this sculptural bag, which is lined with iridescent fabric and, as a pretty finishing touch, embellished with sparkling beads.

Ribbon Evening Bag

you will need
Pleated wire-edged ribbon,
1.6m x 5cm/1⅞yd x 2in
Scissors
Tape measure
Needle and matching thread
Pleated wire-edged ribbon,
40 x 6cm/16 x 2½in
Matching organza fabric
Plate, 14cm/5½in diameter
Pencil
Sewing-machine
Dressmaker's pins
Fine matching cord, 38cm/15in
Decorative glass beads

1 For the main bag, cut eight pieces of 5cm/2in wide pleated ribbon. Using a matching thread, oversew the long edges of the pieces of ribbon together to form a rectangle, then join the two outside edges together to make a cylinder.

2 To make the bottom of the bag, stitch the two ends of the 6cm/2½in wide ribbon together with a 1cm/½in seam. Run a gathering stitch along one edge and pull up tightly. Secure the ends on the wrong side.

3 Slip stitch the outer edge of the bottom of the bag to the lower edge of the side, turning in the raw edges.

4 For the lining, cut a rectangle 18 x 40cm/7 x 16in and a circle with a 7cm/2¾in radius from the organza, using a plate.

5 Machine stitch the side seam, and pin and tack (baste) the side to the bottom of the bag. Machine stitch together.

ribbon evening bag **81**

6 With the wrong sides facing, fit the lining into the bag. Fold in the top edges of both the lining and the ribbon and slip stitch the two together.

7 To make the carriers for the tie, cut two 6cm/2½in lengths of cord and poke the raw ends through a side seam on either side of the bag, 4cm/1½in from the top. Stitch in place. Cut a piece of cord 25cm/10in long, fold it in half and knot the ends.

8 Thread the loop through the carriers and pass the knotted ends through the loop. Hand stitch decorative glass beads around the top edge of the bag at regular intervals.

Whether containing a collection of drawings, school project, or college thesis, this beautiful folder is bound to enhance its contents. The book cloth and lining paper are available from good craft suppliers.

Woven Ribbon Folder

●●●●

you will need
2 pieces of stiff board,
36 x 25cm/14 x 10in
Sheet of artist's black lining paper
PVA (white) glue
Glue spreader or paintbrush
Book cloth or stiffened fabric,
1m x 50cm/1yd x 20in
Pencil
Ruler
Scissors
Wood chisel
Hammer
Piece of wood
Black ribbon, 90cm x 6mm/36 x ⅜in
Iron-on interfacing, 35 x 23cm/14 x 9in
Masking tape
Burgundy fleur-de-lis ribbon,
4.6m x 4cm/5yd x 1½in
Iron

1 Line the two boards with black paper, glueing it in place. To make the gusset, cut an 86 x 10cm/34 x 4in strip of book cloth or stiffened fabric and line it with artist's black paper. Fold the strip in half lengthways, then fold the two halves in half again to create a concertina.

2 Mark a point 27cm/10½in from each end of the strip. Fold the strip lengthways at the first point so that you have a double layer. Carefully cut a triangle out of each corner. Open out, then fold and cut the strip at the other 27cm/10½in point in the same way.

3 Fold the strip at the two 27cm/10½in points so that the two end sections of the gusset strip are at right angles to the middle section.

4 Glue the two boards inside the gusset so the edges lie within the two outermost folds. Press all the creases firmly. Cut two pieces of cloth 5cm/2in longer than the boards and slightly narrower. Stick these to the outside of the boards, leaving the excess at the open edge to be turned over later.

5 Chisel two holes into each side of the top edge of the folder. Protect the boards while you do this by placing a piece of wood between them. Cut the 6mm/¼in ribbon into four equal lengths and thread one through each hole. Turn over the excess lining and glue down to secure the ribbons inside the folder.

6 Tape the interfacing to a weaving board, glue side up. Cut the fleur-de-lis ribbon into eight 27cm/10½in strips and six 40cm/16in strips. Place the eight shorter ribbons side by side over the interfacing and hold them in place with masking tape.

7 Weave the six longer ribbons, plain side up, through the fleur-de-lis ribbons, following the plain-weave technique (see Basic Techniques). Make sure the weaving is even and tight. Press with a dry moderate iron when complete to fuse the ribbon to the interfacing.

8 Trim the edges of the weaving to 2cm/¾in. Fold this allowance over the interfacing and iron carefully. Glue down the edges as necessary, then glue the woven panel to the front of the folder to complete.

Create an heirloom gift for a new baby by combining the freshness of pure white cotton and broderie anglaise with the silky soft appeal of floral ribbon embroidery in delicate pastels.

Ribbon-embroidered Baby Pillow

you will need

White cotton piqué, 90 x 30cm/36 x 12in
Dressmaking scissors
Tape measure
Lightweight iron-on interfacing, 23cm/9in square
Iron
Fabric marker
Embroidery hoop
Chenille needle
Satin ribbon in pale pink, dusky pink, pale mint green, pale lime green and pale aqua, 1.75m x 3mm/ 2yd x ⅛in of each
Narrow broderie anglaise insertion, 1.4m/1½yd
Broderie anglaise edging, 1.4m x 7.5cm/1½yd x 3in
Dressmaker's pins
Needle and matching and contrasting threads
Ribbon, 1.4m x 6mm/1½yd x ¼in
Tapestry needle
Cushion pad, 30cm/12in square

1 Cut a 23cm/9in square of cotton piqué and iron the interfacing to one side. Trace the template at the back of the book and mount in a hoop. For the rose centre, sew a star of four pale pink straight stitches. In dusky pink work a ring of stitches around the star.

2 Work the leaves in straight stitch with the green ribbons and the rosebuds in lazy daisy. Complete the rest of the design using a range of random stitches, and add a bow to the space at the bottom edge. Trim the fabric down a 15cm/6in square.

3 Cut four 9cm/3½in squares and four 15 x 9cm/6 x 3½in pieces of piqué. From the broderie anglaise insertion, cut four 9cm/3½in, two 15cm/6in and two 33cm/13in lengths. Position the pieces and the lace around the embroidered square, following the diagram opposite.

4 Make the front panel by joining the pieces together in three rows with the short lengths of lace insertion, leaving a 1cm/½in seam allowance. Use the two long strips to join the three rows together. Press the seams away from the insertion. Join the two ends of the broderie anglaise edging and run a gathering thread along the raw edge.

ribbon-embroidered baby pillow **85**

5 Fold the edging into four equal sections, marking each quarter division with a small scissor cut. Pin each of these cuts to one corner of the front panel on the right side. Draw up the gathering thread to fit the front panel. Distribute the gathers evenly, allowing a little more fullness at the corners. Pin the broderie anglaise around the outside edge so that it lies on top of the cushion.

6 Tack (baste) and sew in place. Thread the 6mm/¼in ribbon through the insertion using the tapestry needle. Secure each end with a few tacking stitches.

7 Cut a 30cm/12in square of cotton piqué for the panel back. Pin to the right side of the front panel, ensuring that the lace is free of the seam line. Sew around three sides then turn to the right side. Insert the cushion pad and slip stitch the fourth side closed.

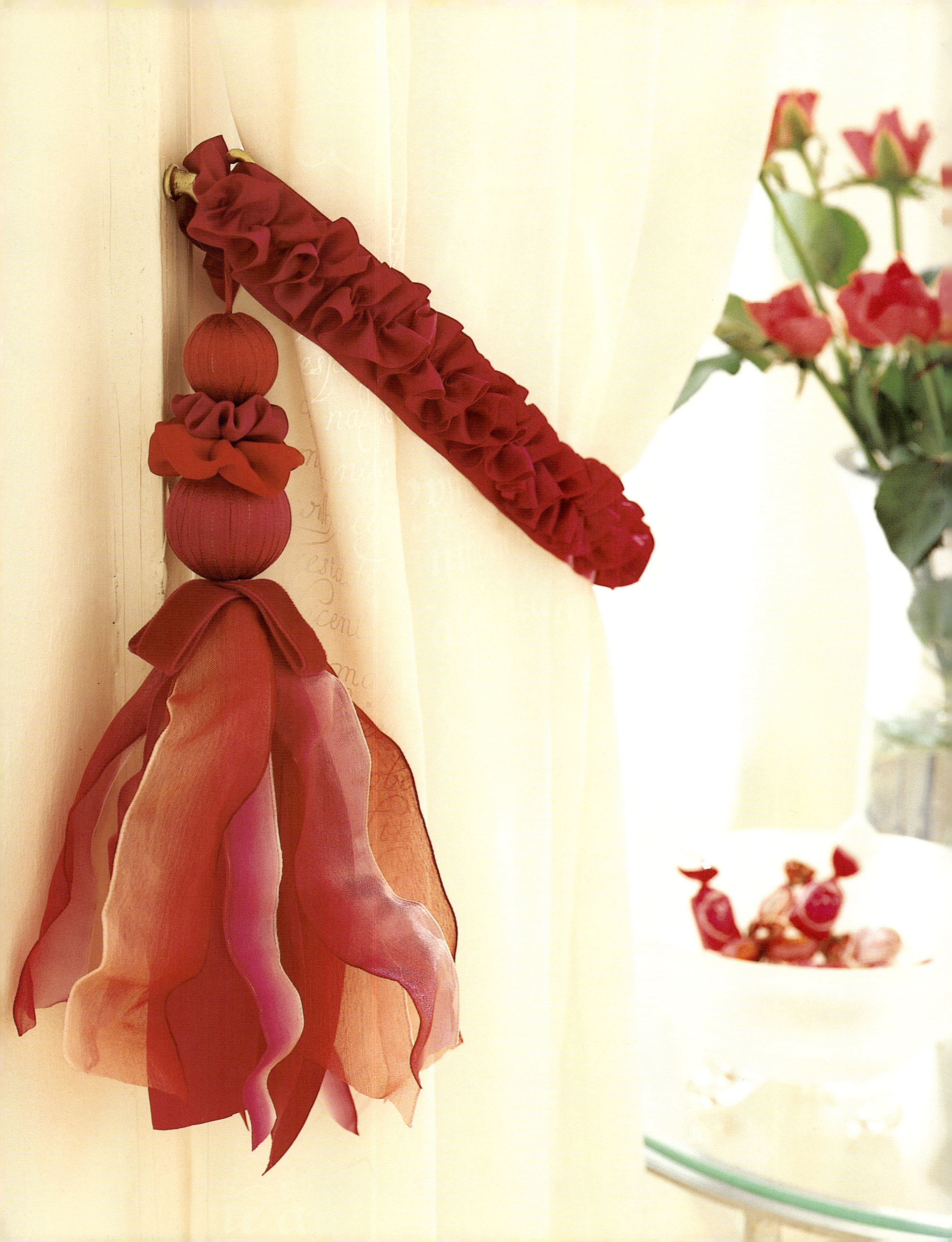

Shocking pink ribbon in a variety of styles – embroidery, satin, velvet and wire-edged – makes up this pretty tie-back. A satin band holds the curtain in place, while the tassel hangs decoratively to one side.

Tasselled Tie-back

you will need
Large-eyed tapestry needle
Narrow embroidery ribbon
Wooden beads in two sizes
Scissors
Selection of satin, velvet and wire-edged ribbons
Needle and strong thread
2 brass rings

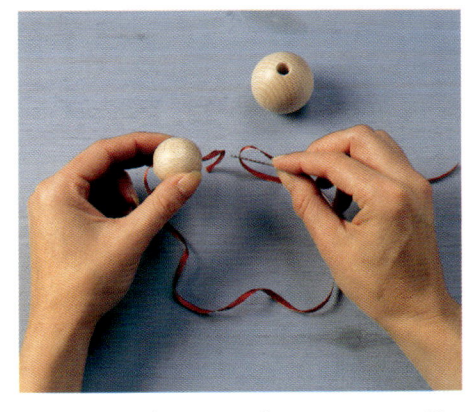

1 Using a large-eyed tapestry needle, thread narrow embroidery ribbon around two large wooden beads to make the tassel head.

2 When the beads are completely covered, tie off the ends securely. Create a hanging loop at the top of the smaller bead.

3 To make a rosette, cut a length of satin ribbon and join the ends neatly together, turning in the raw edges. Work a running stitch along both edges of the ribbon.

4 Gather up the edges tightly to make a puff shape and secure the threads. Make a second rosette, using ribbon of a different width and colour.

▶

5 To make a loop rosette, cut two pieces of narrow velvet ribbon: 30cm/12in lengths will make a rosette that is 15cm/6in across – cut longer lengths for a larger rosette. Fold the raw ends of the first to the centre and secure with a few stitches.

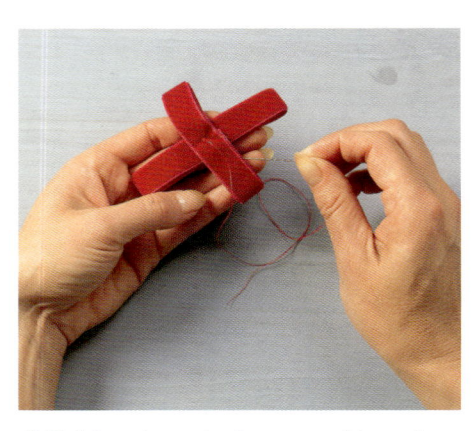

6 Fold and stitch the second length in the same way. Place this loop at right angles across the centre of the first to form a cross, then stitch through all the layers to form the rosette.

7 Select satin and wire-edged ribbons for the skirt of the tassel, cutting them to twice the finished length: this will depend on the size of the tassel head, so experiment until the tassel looks right. Arrange the ribbons in a star shape and secure by stitching through all the layers in the centre.

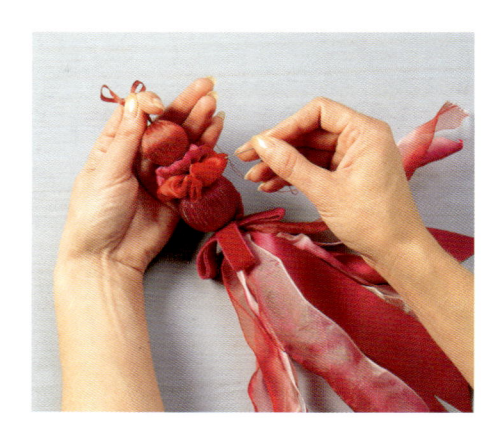

8 To assemble the tassel, thread the large needle with several lengths of strong thread and stitch through the centre of each element, starting with the skirt. Fasten off securely when you reach the top of the smaller bead.

9 To make the tie-back, cut a suitable length of wide satin ribbon. Neaten the raw edges and stitch a brass ring securely to each end. Cut a second piece of the same ribbon twice the length of the tie-back and gather by working a line of running stitches along the centre.

10 Draw up the fullness to fit the foundation ribbon and stitch down the centre. Sew the tassel's hanging loop to one end of the tie-back, so that it will hang at the side of the curtain.

This luxurious little evening bag exudes style and elegance. The velvet is painted with luxurious gold stripes, then woven through with complementary coloured ribbons.

Classic Evening Purse

●●●●

you will need
Black velvet, 40cm/16in square
Black lining fabric, 20cm/8in square
Scissors
Large sheet of paper
Masking tape, 2.5cm/1in wide
Gold fabric paint
Paintbrush
Thin card (stock)
Fabric marker
Small sharp-pointed scissors
Silver ribbon, 1.6m x 6mm/1¾yd x ¼in
Green ribbon, 1.75m x 6mm/2yd x ¼in
Maroon ribbon, 1.75m x 6mm/2yd x ¼in
Tape measure
Tapestry needle
Dressmaker's pins
Needle and matching threads
Iron

1 Enlarge the three pattern pieces at the back of the book to size. A seam allowance of 1cm/12in is included. Cut two of the larger rectangles from black velvet, two of the smaller rectangles from the black lining fabric and one circle from each fabric.

2 Place one rectangle of velvet fabric face up on a sheet of paper (to protect the work surface). Lay vertical strips of masking tape over the velvet, leaving a gap of 2.5cm/1in between them. Lay a double strip of masking tape across the centre of the fabric.

3 Apply gold paint lightly and evenly to the exposed areas of fabric with a dry brush. Leave to dry completely, then peel off the tape carefully. Follow the manufacturer's instructions for fixing the paint.

4 Make a template for the ribbon insertion, cutting points from a strip of card cut to the length of the painted stripes. Mark six evenly spaced points along one edge of the strip. Transfer these points to the velvet with a fabric marker along both sides of each painted strip. Mark only the bottom half of the whole piece of velvet.

▶

5 Use sharp scissors to cut 6mm/¼in slits in the fabric at the marked points. Cut the ribbons into 20cm/8in lengths. Use a tapestry needle to thread one through each row of slits, alternating the colour with each row. Thread the ribbon loosely, allowing it to fall naturally.

6 Secure the ends of each ribbon on the back of the velvet with a few stitches. Repeat steps two to six with the second rectangle of black fabric to make the other half of the bag.

7 With right sides facing, pin, tack (baste) and sew the long sides of the two rectangles together, leaving a space in each seam where indicated on the pattern. Sew both lining rectangles together along the short edges, leaving a gap in one seam for turning.

8 With right sides facing, pin, tack and sew the long sides of the lining to the upper edge of the bag, matching up the seam lines. Press lightly and stitch the seam.

9 Turn the bag inside out and, with right sides facing, pin, tack and sew the circle of velvet to the bottom edge of the bag. Join the circle of lining fabric to the bottom edges of the lining. Turn the bag through the opening to the right side. Fold along the fold line and press gently.

10 Tack along the stitching lines indicated on the pattern to form the drawstring channel, then stitch. Close the side opening with slip stitch (see Basic Stitching Techniques). Thread the remaining ribbon through the channel and tie the ends together to form a drawstring.

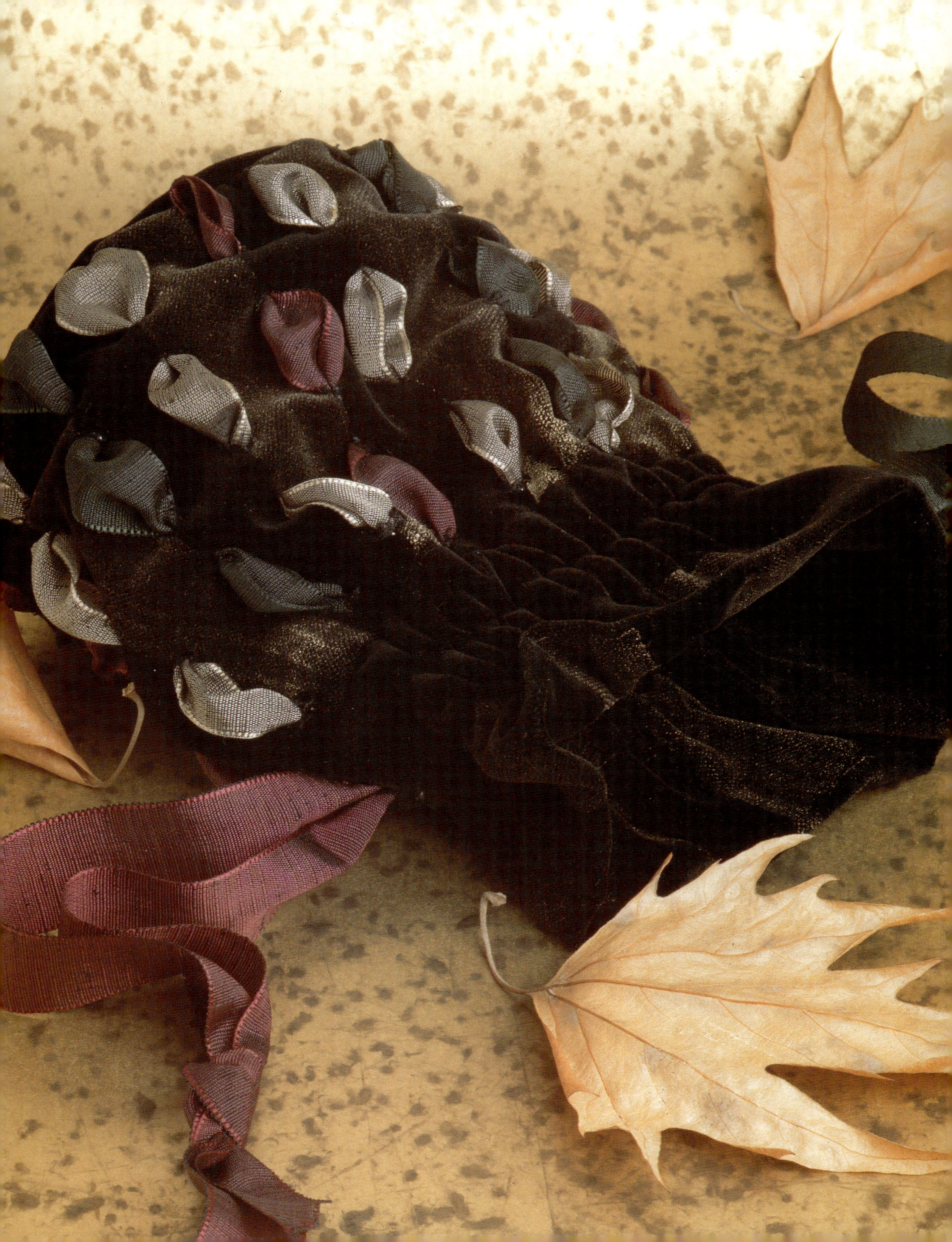

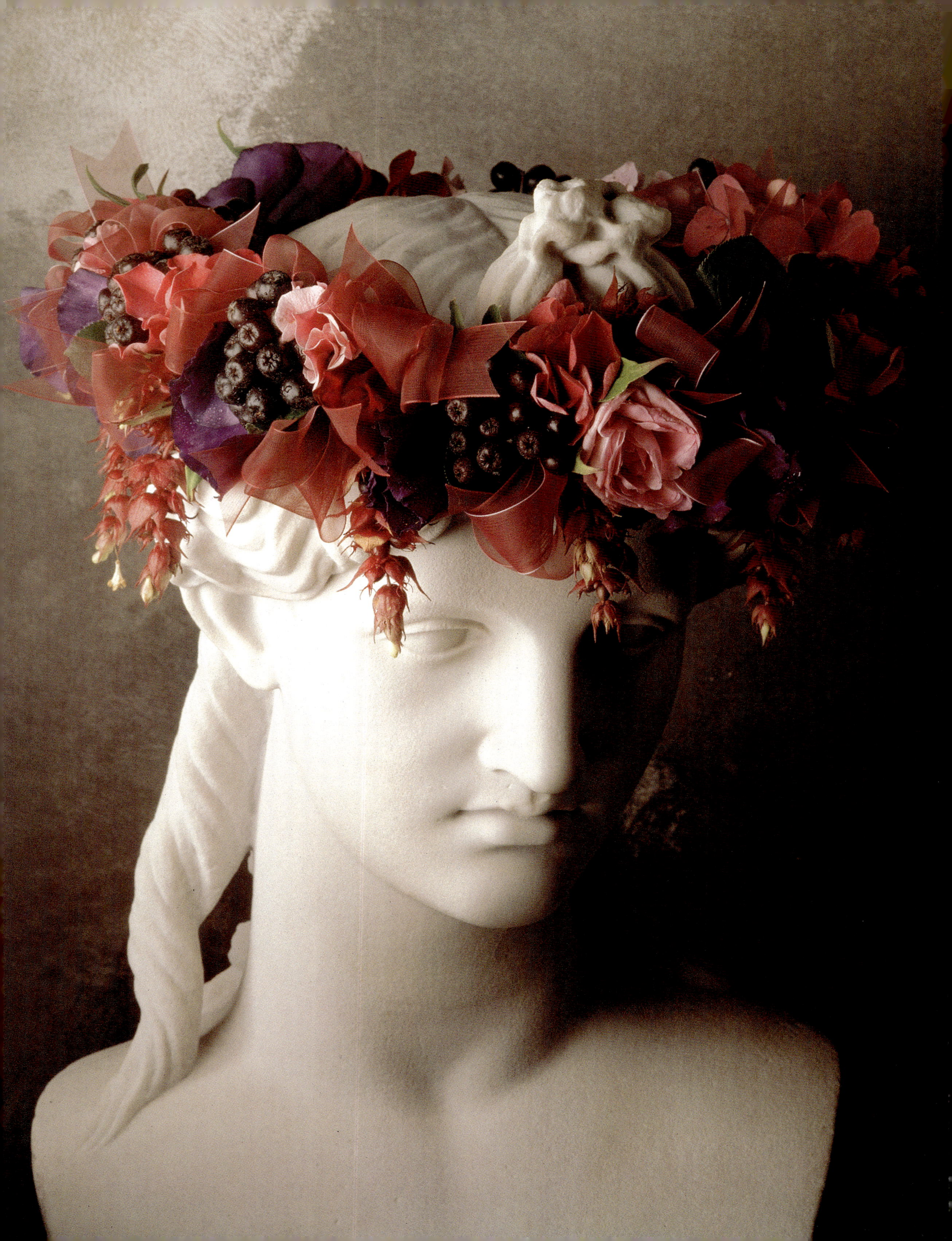

The beautiful blooms that make up this romantic coronet will require special care to keep them pristine: give them a long drink before use and mist the finished headdress lightly with a water spray.

Flower and Ribbon Headdress

●●●●

you will need
12 small clusters of *Aronia melanocarpa* berries
Scissors
Stub (floral) wire, 0.38mm/28g
12 small clusters of hydrangea florets
12 *Leycesteria formosa* flower heads
Small garden roses
12 Lizianthus flower heads
12 single Antirrhinum florets
Florist's tape (stem wrap)
Burgundy sheer ribbon, 8m x 23mm/ 8¾yd x ⅞in
Tape measure
Stub wire, 0.71mm/22g

1 Trim the berry stems. Cut short lengths of fine stub wire to double leg mount them. Holding the stem between finger and thumb, place a wire behind and at a right angle to the stem, one third of the way up. Bend it into a "U" so that one leg is twice as long as the other.

2 Holding the short leg against the stem, wrap the long leg twice around both the stem and the other wire. Straighten both legs, which should now be about equal and in line with the stem. Mount the roses, hydrangeas and leycesteria in the same way.

3 Wire each lizianthus flower head by piercing the seedbox with a length of stub wire. Push it about one third of the way through, then bend the wire legs down and wrap the legs around the stem as described for double leg mounting in step 1.

4 Remove the flower heads of the antirrhinum from the main stem and cut two short stub wires for each one. Fold one wire in half and twist into a loop at the bend. Push the legs down through the throat of the flower and out at the base to create a stem.

94 ribbonwork projects

5 The loop will sit in the narrowest part of the flower, preventing the wire from pulling all the way through. Use the second piece of wire to double leg mount the protruding wires and any natural stem that remains, as shown in steps 1 and 2.

6 Cover all the stems and wires with florist's tape. Hold the end against the top of the stem. With the other hand, hold the rest of the tape at an angle to the stem. Slowly rotate the stem and, keeping the tape taut so that it stretches slightly, wrap it in a downwards spiral, overlapping and pressing it in place.

7 Make 14 three-loop ribbon bows, each with two tails. For each bow, cut a 55cm/22in length of ribbon and divide it into six equal sections. Fold the ribbon accordion-style, pinching the folds together at the base. Double leg mount each bow using stub wire.

8 Cut several equal lengths of heavy stub wire to make the headdress foundation. Group four wires together so each overlaps the next by 3cm/1¼in. Starting at one end, bind them together with florist's tape. As the tape reaches the end of the first wire, add in another length.

9 Continue in this way until the wire measures 3cm/1¼in more than the circumference of the wearer's head. Tape the wired flowers and ribbons to the foundation in your chosen arrangement. Continue to within 3cm/1¼in of the end, curving the wire as you work.

10 Overlap the undecorated end of the stay wire with the decorated beginning. Tape the wires together under the flowers.

Templates

Enlarge the templates on a photocopier. Alternatively, trace the design and draw a grid of evenly spaced squares over the tracing. Draw a larger grid on to another piece of paper and copy the outline square by square. Draw over the lines to make sure they are continuous.

Baby Pillow p84–5

Embroidered Basket p40–1

Acknowledgements

The publisher would like to thank the following people for the projects and photography in this book:

LISA BROWN, Luxurious Giftwrapping 28, Rosy Lampshade 30, Pillowcase Edgings 32, Embroidered Basket 40, Ribbon Door Curtain 44, Ribboned Throw 48, Striped Ribbon Cushion 50, Ribbon-rose Coat Hangers 61, Appliquéd Ribbon Café Curtain 71, Deck-chair Cover 74, Woven Ribbon Headboard 78, Ribbon Evening Bag 80, Tasselled Tie-back 87,
LUCINDA GANDERTON, Ribbon Hat Box 63.
CHRISTINE KINGDOM, Ballet Shoes 26, Gift Boxes 35, Bathroom Set 36, Ribbon-embroidered Bag 38, Ribbon Table Mats 42, Golden Braid Cushion 46, Sunflower-motif Jacket 52, Ribbon Jewellery 54, Tartan Ribbon Roses 56, Ribbon Lantern 58, Ribbon Christmas Decorations 69, Basket-weave Cushion 76, Woven Ribbon Folder 82, Ribbon-embroidered Baby Pillow 84, Classic Evening Purse 89, Flower and Ribbon Headdress 93
ISABEL STANLEY, Satin and Velvet Ribbon Shade 66

Photography: Lizzie Orme, Michelle Garrett, Lucinda Symons, Peter Williams.

Index

appliqué work:
 ribbon café curtain 71–3
Ashby, Daphne J. 13

bags:
 evening purse 89–91
 ribbon evening 80–1
 ribbon-embroidered 38–9
ballet shoes 26–7
Banham, Jenny 12
baskets, ribbonwork 40–1
bathroom sets, ribbonwork 36–7
bows, ribbonwork 18
Brown, Lindsay Chalford 14
Buckler, Jo 12

café curtain, appliqué ribbon 71–3
check ribbons 17
Chippindale, Jenny 14
christening gowns 12
Christmas decorations: 68–70
coat hangers, ribbon-rose 60–2
curtains:
 ribbon door 44–5
 tiebacks 86–8
cushions:
 basket-weave 76–7

 golden braid 46–7
 striped ribbon 50–1
cut-edge craft ribbon 16

deck-chair covers 74–5
door curtain 92–3
 ribbon 44–5

evening bags, ribbon 80–1
evening purses 89–91
flower motifs 52–3, 56–7, 92–4
folders, woven ribbon 82–3

gift boxes, ribbonwork 34–5
giftwrapping, ribbonwork 28–9
gloves, ribbonwork 13
grosgrain ribbon 16

hat boxes, ribbon 63–5
hats, ribbonwork 12
headboards, woven ribbon 78–9
headresses, flower and ribbon 92–4
history of ribbonwork 10–11

jackets, sun-flower motif 52–3
jaquards 16
lace-edged satins 16

lampshades:
 ribbonwork 30–1
 satin and velvet ribbon 66–7
lanterns, ribbon 58–9

merrow-edged ribbons 16–7
metallic ribbons 17
moiré ribbons 17

Noguchi, Hikaru 14

ombré taffeta ribbons 17

patchwork weave ribbonwork 21
pillowcases:
 ribbon-embroidered baby 84–5
plaid ribbons 17
pompom bows 18
purses, evening 89–91

ribbon types 16–7
ribbonwork 10–23
 stitching 22–3
 techniques 18–73
roses:
 ribbonwork 169
 tartan ribbon 56–7

satin ribbons 17
sheer ribbons 17
shot-effect taffeta ribbons 17
stitching, ribbonwork 22–3
sunflower-motif jacket 52–3

table mats, ribbon 42–3
techniques, ribbonwork 18–73
templates 95

throw:
 ribboned 48–9
tie-backs
 tasselled 86–8
Tindale, Patricia 12

velvet:
 ribbons 17
Voisey, M. Maureen 14

wallhangings, ribbonwork 12
weaving:
 ribbonwork 20–1
wire-edged taffeta ribbons 17
Woods, Pamela 13
woven-edge ribbon 17

zigzag weave, ribbonwork 21